baking
out loud

out

baking loud

fun desserts with big flavors

hedy goldsmith

WITH ABIGAIL JOHNSON DODGE

CLARKSON POTTER/PUBLISHERS

NEW YORK

Copyright © 2012 by Hedy Goldsmith
Photographs copyright © 2012 by Ben Fink,
with the exception of photos on page 7
© 2012 by Michael Pisarri and page 224
© 2012 by Ryan Oswald

Published in the United States by Clarkson
Potter/Publishers, an imprint of the Crown
Publishing Group, a division of Random
House, Inc., New York.
www.crownpublishing.com
www.clarksonpotter.com

CLARKSON POTTER is a trademark and
POTTER with colophon is a registered
trademark of Random House, Inc.

Library of Congress Cataloging-in-
Publication Data
   Goldsmith, Hedy.
   Baking Out Loud / Hedy Goldsmith.
      p.   cm.
   Includes index.
   1. Desserts.   2. Cooking.
3. Confectionery.
4. Cookbooks.   I. Title.
   TX773.G56 2012
   641.86—dc23
2011042268

ISBN 978-0-307-95177-9
eISBN 978-0-7704-3341-3

Printed in China

Book and Jacket design by
Stephanie Huntwork
Jacket photographs by Ben Fink

10 9 8 7 6 5 4 3 2 1

First Edition

contents

introduction

My mom was no Suzy Homemaker. She was a working mom who actually entertained the idea of turning our kitchen into a library. If fast food is at one end of the spectrum and slow food at the other, the Goldsmith household in Philadelphia bolted ahead at a gallop. Our pantry was always filled with the latest convenience foods: SpaghettiOs, Pop-Tarts, Chips Ahoy! cookies. I grew up thinking that everyone ate dinner out of three-compartment aluminum trays.

My earliest "cooking" adventures involved these supermarket goodies, and the kitchen quickly became my playground, the Easy-Bake Oven my babysitter. I remember at a young age dipping Charles Chips into half-melted Hershey's bars for a salty-sweet treat and topping my vanilla ice cream with Cap'n Crunch cereal. I was a curious, chubby kid who was drawn to the bright packaging of junk foods. I would amuse myself for hours organizing all the mini pots and pans and alphabetizing the boxes of cake mix. I should have guessed my future then, but the only lightbulb that went off was the one cooking my first batch of brownies. Then again, I was only six years old.

My mom had quite a sweet tooth. She and I would go on road trips to Entenmann's bakery outlet on Academy Road in the Far Northeast of Philly to buy coffee cakes and pound cakes by the dozen. When we ran out of our stockpiled goods, we'd walk hand in hand the two blocks to Castor Bakery. Some moms teach their daughters how to shop for just the right pair of shoes. Not mine. With my face pressed against the glass counter at Castor, I learned how to scrutinize every crumb on each Jewish babka to find perfection.

When I was in fourth grade, I became a Girl Scout, and cookies came into my life in a big way. I wanted to be the Girl Scout who sold the most cookies ever—and I did, at least in Philadelphia, which won me a trip to Washington, DC. That's the power of Thin Mints. By the time I was in high school, I was making chocolate-covered pretzels for my friends on the softball team—not your run-of-the-mill variety but the triple-dipped kind.

I loved making people happy with food, but I never thought about baking for a living. Instead, I went to the Philadelphia College of Art and was a photography and film major with a minor in graphic design. Then one day I stumbled upon Reading Terminal Market in downtown Philly, a magical place filled with things I had never seen before, let alone tasted. Suddenly I caught the cooking bug, and I knew I wanted to do it for a living.

After graduation, I somehow landed an interview at a restaurant in Center City. Though I didn't really know what I was doing, I got a job as a prep cook reporting to the kitchen manager, Melanie. After many months of perfecting coleslaw and tartar sauce, I was finally allowed to help Mel with desserts. She gave me a baking book to take home so that I could study up. Maida who?

Every night, I would go home and try to follow one of the recipes in that cookbook. The

next morning I would get to work with note cards in hand, on the off chance I would be asked to break out a dessert. Finally, Melanie asked me to make something chocolate. To impress her, I chose one of the most difficult cakes in the book: Queen Mother's Cake, a flourless chocolate cake with ground almonds. The tricky part of this cake was whipping the egg whites just right and folding them into the cake batter so as not to lose volume. Melanie was indeed impressed. Maida Heatter's *Book of Great Desserts* would ultimately change my life.

It was soon after I discovered Maida that my mother died suddenly, in her sleep, when I was way too young. My life was just starting, and I had lost my best friend and my biggest supporter. My mom never tasted a single dessert of mine, aside from the brownies from the Easy-Bake Oven. It remains the biggest disappointment in my life that I never got to bake for her. Heartbroken, and with nothing to lose, I applied and was accepted to the Culinary Institute of America in Hyde Park, New York, which had just started a new baking and pastry program. I packed up my cookbooks and snow globe collection and moved to Poughkeepsie.

In cake and torte classes, my creative mind started churning at warp speed. Candy making and working with chocolate required such patience, such focus, and I learned from the best in the field. And it turned out that everything I had studied in art school gave me a competitive edge in culinary school. My ability to look at the endless possibilities of a blank canvas served me well when it came to staring down a blank dessert plate.

After graduation, I took a job at the Waldorf Astoria in New York, where I certainly paid my dues. We did a lot of high-volume production, and I remember cakes baking in a deck oven that had been built at the turn of the century. Five foot two and a hundred and eight pounds, I could barely hold the heavy peel used to remove the cakes, or, even on tippy-toes, see into the oven. And I had no help. My coworkers were seasoned old guys who, frankly, enjoyed watching me struggle. The job was hell. I loved Manhattan, the people, the sights, the sounds, the food—but it was time to make a big change. After a year and a half, I gave in to the lure of the beach. I vacationed in Florida, loved it, and secured a job as soon as I could.

Funny, but I never knew my hair was wavy until I stepped off the plane at Miami International Airport. I also never knew that in Miami, Maida would reenter my life—though this time in person—to once again guide my career.

I worked as the catering director at the glamorous CenTrust Tower in downtown Miami before becoming the pastry chef at Mark Militello's restaurant, Mark's Place, in North Miami. Maida happened to live near the restaurant and loved coming for lunch. One day, she asked to meet the pastry chef. I was so nervous at finally meeting the undisputed Queen of Sweets! Maida was beyond kind, showering me with praise during that first meeting. She invited me to lunch at her friend Michael Schwartz's new restaurant in South Beach, called Nemo, and we had great fun chatting about all things pastry. Since Maida knew Mark was moving his signature restaurant to Fort Lauderdale, she asked what I wanted to do next. I didn't hesitate to say I would love working at Nemo, and not twenty-four hours passed before I received a phone call from Michael.

Michael and I connected immediately. His approach to food is all about pared-down simplicity and letting the ingredients speak for themselves. It just so happens that by then my desserts at Mark's were going from overly sophisticated to simple, but with in-your-face flavors. Nemo was slammed and kept receiving more and more accolades while I worked there, including two very special ones from critics at the *New York Times* lauding my desserts.

Then Michael decided to leave Nemo. After helping owner Myles Chefetz open what became South Beach's glitziest restaurant, Prime 112. I left to develop a line of packaged goods. At about that time, Michael opened his namesake restaurant, Michael's Genuine Food & Drink, in Miami's Design District. When Michael asked me to work with him again full-time, I jumped in as the pastry chef soon after the restaurant opened and never looked back. Frank Bruni, the *New York Times* food critic at the time, called Michael's one of the top ten new restaurants in the country and then followed that piece with another one singing the praises of our Sunday brunch. Not only did he dream about my Pop T's, he said he would come back to Miami just for them. He called me sly and nostalgic and said he loved "anything and everything the pastry chef, Hedy Goldsmith, whips up." I have never felt so flattered.

I make sweets for a living, and I couldn't imagine a life without baking and making people happy. My whole life has influenced the desserts that I make, and those early salty-sweet memories and big flavors still shape my palate. You can see

my love for junk food in the Childhood Treats chapter, where the recipes are my homage to the fast, fatty, calorie-driven, chemically enhanced goodies from my past. But all of them—like Red Velvet Twinks (page 19), Overstuffed Nutters (page 43), and Pop T's (page 12)—are reconceived using real ingredients, the names of which you can pronounce. Since so many people rave about my ice creams, I've devoted a whole chapter to frozen things. I'd say the Bacon Maple Pecan Ice Cream (page 160), Buttered Popcorn Gelato (page 163), and South Philly Lemon Ice (page 158) make me the happiest. But what I've always loved most is baking cookies, and my all-time favorites are Anise Almond Biscotti (page 88).

Desserts make everything seem right in the world, even if for a moment. I hope you'll taste joy in these desserts and experience the thrill of sharing that with others. Don't forget to add a good sprinkling of my secret ingredient: passion. Use enough of it and you'll see what I mean about making people happy.

child treats

hood

Pop t's

MAKES 16 Long before the fancy flavors and elaborate decoration of today's Pop-Tarts, there was old-school simplicity. I remember dragging a chair halfway across my kitchen floor so I could reach high up in the cabinet—way in the back, hidden behind the "healthy" breakfast stuff—and grab my favorite Pop-Tart: brown sugar and cinnamon. Too excited to wait for the toaster to warm it up, I would eat the dough edges in an organized pattern moving clockwise around the tart, then the top layer, and finally the bottom layer with the filling. Nirvana. Now that I'm older, I've re-created my favorite breakfast treat with an adult pastry chef spin (and kids like them too!).

3 cups all-purpose flour

2 tablespoons granulated sugar

2 teaspoons kosher salt

1 cup (2 sticks) unsalted butter, cut into cubes and very cold

7 tablespoons ice water

1½ teaspoons white vinegar

1 extra-large egg, at room temperature

¾ cup Pop Jam (page 205) or good-quality store-bought jam

⅓ cup turbinado sugar

1 Using an electric mixer fitted with the paddle attachment, mix the flour, sugar, and salt until blended. Add the butter, and mix on medium-low speed for 4 minutes, or until very small pieces of butter are visible. Combine 6 tablespoons of the ice water and the vinegar and add it to the flour mixture. Mix on medium speed until moist crumbles of dough form.

2 Scrape the dough and any remaining flour onto a work surface and knead 6 to 8 times, until the mixture comes together in a smooth dough. Do not overwork the dough or the Pop T's will be tough.

3 Divide the dough in half (weigh the halves if you have a scale). Then shape both halves into flat, even rectangles and cover one in plastic wrap so that it doesn't dry out.

4 Put a large piece of parchment paper on a work surface. Put the unwrapped rectangle of dough on the center and top it with another sheet of parchment paper. Roll the dough into a ⅛-inch-thick rectangle slightly larger

(RECIPE CONTINUES)

than 14 × 10 inches, stopping occasionally to peel away the paper, dust the dough lightly with flour, and reposition the paper so you don't get any wrinkles. Try to keep the rectangle shape nice and neat—this will help you keep the Pop T count accurate.

5 Slide the dough in the parchment sheets onto a baking sheet and refrigerate for 30 to 45 minutes, until the dough is very firm. If you want to chill the dough faster, freeze for about 15 minutes. Repeat with remaining dough.

6 Line 2 baking sheets with parchment paper or nonstick liners. Combine the egg with the remaining 1 tablespoon ice water in a small bowl, and mix with a fork until blended.

7 Working with one sheet of dough at a time, arrange them on a work surface and peel away the top parchment. Using a ruler and a small, sharp knife or a pizza cutter, trim the dough sheets to 10 × 14-inch rectangles. Cut each one into sixteen 2½ × 3½-inch rectangles.

8 Using a metal spatula, carefully lift 16 rectangles from the parchment and arrange them about 1 inch apart on the prepared baking sheets. Fill a pastry bag (no tip needed) with the jam, pipe a scant tablespoon down the center of each rectangle, and spread the jam to about ½ inch from the edge of each rectangle. (You can also use a spoon to do this, but I think it's faster and easier to use a pastry bag.) Brush the borders with the beaten egg.

My Crimper: I've adapted one of my old forks into the perfect crimping tool for Pop T's. Bend the bottom third of the fork tines to a 90-degree angle—you might need a Vise-Grip or a very strong human for this project. It makes for quick and easy crimping.

The filled pop tarts can be frozen before baking for up to 1 month. Thaw overnight in the refrigerator before baking as directed.

9 Carefully place the remaining rectangles over the jam and gently press out all the air. If you want perfect-looking pop tarts, use a small knife to trim off any uneven edges. Using the tines of a fork, crimp the edges to seal. Cover the tarts with plastic wrap and slide the baking sheets back into the refrigerator for 1 to 2 hours, or freeze again for 30 minutes to 1 hour, until the dough is very firm. Cover and refrigerate the remaining egg mixture.

10 Position racks in the upper middle and lower middle of the oven, and preheat the oven to 350°F (325°F if using a convection oven).

11 Using a small knife, cut three small (½-inch) slits in the top of each pop tart; brush with the remaining beaten egg, and sprinkle with the turbinado sugar. Bake for 34 to 36 minutes (20 to 23 minutes if using a convection oven), until the bottoms are golden brown.

12 Transfer the baking sheets to wire racks and let cool. You'll be tempted to eat the tarts right out of the oven but DON'T! The jam is nuclear hot at this point.

13 Store the tarts in an airtight container at room temperature for up to 3 days and reheat in a toaster.

you've got chocolate in my peanut butter bars

MAKES 20 PIECES This is my all-time favorite guilty pleasure that makes everything right with the world. The best candy on the planet. Hands down.

Flashback to when I was five years old, living in Northeast Philadelphia, and it was Halloween. My mom made me a fussy clown costume that I could barely move in. After trick-or-treating, my brother, Steven, and I dumped our bags of candy on the dining room table. Mom allowed us to keep only our favorite candies, and she would take everything else to work to share with her coworkers (though I'm not certain she really shared!). The choosing was brutal, but when I got to that bright orange package of Reese's Peanut Butter Cups, nothing else really mattered.

My version of the classic has a rich peanut butter flavor and is silky smooth in texture. Leftovers, if you have any, make a killer sundae topping.

8 ounces bittersweet chocolate (preferably Valrhona Caraïbe 66%)

6 tablespoons (¾ stick) unsalted butter, at room temperature

⅓ cup (packed) dark brown sugar

1 cup confectioners' sugar

1 teaspoon kosher salt

1 cup creamy peanut butter (preferably organic), at room temperature

1 Line the bottom and sides of an 8½ × 4½-inch loaf pan with parchment paper or foil, and grease it lightly (preferably with Pam). Melt the chocolate in a small heatproof bowl set over simmering water, stirring until the chocolate is smooth, about 4 minutes. Remove from the heat and let cool slightly.

2 Using an electric mixer fitted with the paddle attachment, beat the butter, brown sugar, confectioners' sugar, and salt on medium speed for about 3 minutes, or until blended and smooth. Add the peanut butter, and mix until just blended.

3 Scrape the mixture into the prepared loaf pan, and using an offset spatula, spread it evenly. Place plastic wrap directly onto the peanut butter mixture, and press to smooth the top. Refrigerate for 2 to 3 hours, until very cold, or freeze for 45 to 60 minutes.

(RECIPE CONTINUES)

4 Using the parchment paper or foil liner of the loaf pan, transfer the candy onto a work surface. Peel away the paper or foil, and invert the rectangle onto a cutting board or plate. Using a large knife, trim off the edges to make an even-edged rectangle (nibble on them—so good). Pour the melted chocolate over the top, and spread it evenly. Refrigerate for 2 hours, until very cold.

5 To serve, cut the candy lengthwise into two 1½-inch-wide strips. Cut each strip into 10 pieces. Store in an airtight container in the refrigerator for up to 5 days. Make sure to serve chilled.

VARIATION

This recipe also makes a crazy-good peanut butter s'more. Spread homemade Cinnamon Graham Crackers (page 85) with room-temperature peanut butter filling, add a toasted homemade Marshmallow (page 41) and a drizzle of Best-Ever Chocolate Sauce (page 214), and top with another graham.

red velvet twinks

MAKES 16 Twinkies are another favorite from my childhood, and this recipe makes a similar snack cake with a southern twist. My first red velvet experience came many years into my career as a pastry chef. Working in Miami, I quickly became familiar with this local favorite, and the classic Twinkie has benefited from my conversion. Goat cheese adds a wonderful tang to the traditional cream cheese filling and elevates it to a whole new level.

FOR THE CAKES

2½ cups cake flour

2 tablespoons natural dark cocoa powder (preferably Valrhona)

1 teaspoon kosher salt

1½ cups sugar

1½ cups canola oil

2 extra-large eggs, at room temperature

2 teaspoons vanilla bean paste or pure vanilla extract

1 teaspoon red food coloring gel (or 2 teaspoons liquid coloring)

1 cup buttermilk, at room temperature

2 teaspoons white vinegar

1½ teaspoons baking soda

1 To make the cakes, position racks in the upper middle and lower middle of the oven, and preheat the oven to 350°F (325°F if using a convection oven). Lightly grease (preferably with Pam) 2 canoe baking pans. (Similar to muffin tins, these pans have 8 oblong cups with rounded bottoms. You can buy them in gourmet equipment or bakeware shops or online.)

2 Sift the flour, cocoa powder, and salt together.

3 Using an electric mixer fitted with the whisk attachment, beat the sugar and oil on medium speed until blended. Add the eggs, vanilla, and food coloring and beat on medium speed for 1 minute, until blended. Add a third of the flour mixture, and beat on low speed until just blended. Add half of the buttermilk and mix on low speed until just blended. Repeat with the remaining flour mixture and buttermilk, ending with the last third of the flour mixture, mixing until the dough just comes together.

4 Stir the vinegar and baking soda together in a small bowl. Add to the batter and stir using a rubber spatula until just blended.

(RECIPE CONTINUES)

FOR THE FILLING

4 ounces cream cheese, at room temperature

4 ounces goat cheese, at room temperature

6 tablespoons (¾ stick) unsalted butter, at room temperature

1½ cups confectioners' sugar

1 teaspoon vanilla bean paste or pure vanilla extract

½ teaspoon kosher salt

2 cups chopped toasted pecans or shredded coconut

Try adding some chopped-up Bacon Praline (page 212) to the filling.

5 Divide the batter evenly between the prepared baking pans. Bake for 17 to 19 minutes (14 to 17 minutes if using a convection oven), switching the baking pans' positions halfway through baking, until the tops feel slightly firm and a toothpick inserted in the center of one cake comes out clean. Transfer the baking pans to wire racks and let cool completely.

6 To make the filling, using an electric mixer fitted with the paddle attachment, beat the cream cheese, goat cheese, and butter on medium speed for about 2 minutes, until soft and smooth. Add the confectioners' sugar, vanilla, and salt, and beat on medium-high speed for 2 minutes, until smooth, light, and fluffy.

7 Scrape three-quarters of the filling into a piping bag fitted with a ¼-inch plain tip, leaving the remaining quarter of the icing in the bowl for use in the next step.

8 Because the round top of these cakes actually becomes the bottom, you'll want to trim off this rounded part using a serrated knife. To fill, hold a cake in one hand, flat side up, and push the tip of the pastry bag into the flat side of the cake about 1 inch from the end. Squeeze about 1 tablespoon of filling into the cake. Repeat 2 more times, evenly spacing the filling across the cake. Using a small spatula, cover the bottom with a thin layer of the remaining icing. Dip the bottom into the pecans or coconut, and arrange, rounded side up, on a serving plate. Repeat with the remaining cakes. Serve immediately or store in an airtight container in the refrigerator for up to 3 days.

tootses

MAKES ABOUT 24 (2-INCH) ROLLS When I was at the Culinary Institute of America, I was learning to make old-fashioned and out-of-date ornate cake ornaments. After tasting the modeling chocolate I was using, I realized it tasted just like Tootsie Rolls. Problem was, I couldn't possibly think of a bride who would want a cake decorated with Tootsie Rolls. So I worked on them some and came up with this recipe. They're not the Tootsies you grew up with but are way better. I like to serve these wrapped up in foil for a retro, cute, and really-easy-to-make treat.

7 ounces bittersweet chocolate (preferably Valrhona Caraïbe 66%), chopped

¼ cup Lyle's Golden Syrup (found in most grocery stores)

1 Melt the chocolate in a small heatproof bowl set over simmering water, stirring until the chocolate is melted and smooth. Remove the bowl from the heat and set aside for 3 minutes to cool slightly. The chocolate should be about 110°F.

2 Stir in the syrup until just blended. Cover the bowl with plastic wrap and set aside at room temperature for about 1 hour, or until the candy is firm but still malleable. If you want to speed things along, put the bowl in the refrigerator and stir every 2 to 3 minutes, keeping an eye on it since it will firm up very quickly.

3 Dump the candy onto a work surface and divide it into thirds (the portions don't need to be exactly even). Working with one third at a time (cover the rest with plastic wrap), use your hands to knead the chocolate until it is soft and pliable (kind of like Play-Doh).

4 Roll the chocolate into a long rope about ½ inch in diameter. Using a small knife, cut the roll into 2-inch-long pieces. Wrap them individually in foil, candy wrappers, or waxed paper. Repeat with the remaining chocolate. Store the rolls at room temperature for up to 2 weeks—though I don't think they'll last that long.

MAKES 1 POUND

Bark, **noun:** Tough protective covering of the woody stems of trees.

Popcorn + Peanut Bark, **noun:** Delicious dark chocolate covering protecting buttery, salty, freshly popped popcorn and peanuts.

Bark, **verb:** Speak in an unfriendly tone when it's all gone.

12 ounces bittersweet chocolate, (preferably Valrhona Caraïbe 66%), chopped

3 cups freshly popped popcorn (page 53)

½ cup salted peanuts (preferably Virginia)

Pinch of kosher salt

1 Line a baking sheet with a nonstick liner.

2 Melt the chocolate in a large heatproof bowl set over simmering water, stirring until the chocolate is melted and smooth, about 4 minutes. Remove the bowl from the heat and add the popcorn, peanuts, and salt. Fold the mixture until the popcorn and peanuts are evenly coated with the chocolate.

3 Scrape the mixture onto the prepared baking sheet and spread into a thin layer.

4 Refrigerate for about 30 minutes, or until cold and firm. Break into small clusters and store in an airtight container in the refrigerator for up to 5 days.

whoopie pies

MAKES 16 "PIES" Every summer, my family would take a car trip along the coast-line of Maine. When I was very young, we would make this journey without air-conditioning. It was crazy hot. I dreaded the travel but loved the reward at the end of that long, hot trip: we'd stop at Labadies' Bakery in Lewiston, Maine (it's been there since 1925), for the most amazingly sweet, light, and fluffy whoopie pies.

FOR THE CAKES

- 2 cups all-purpose flour
- ½ cup natural dark cocoa powder (preferably Valrhona)
- 1 tablespoon finely ground espresso beans
- ½ teaspoon baking soda
- 1 teaspoon ground cinnamon (preferably Saigon, see note, page 69)
- ½ cup (1 stick) unsalted butter, at room temperature
- 1 cup (packed) dark brown sugar
- 1 teaspoon kosher salt
- 1 extra-large egg, at room temperature
- 1 teaspoon vanilla bean paste or pure vanilla extract
- 1 cup buttermilk (not low-fat), at room temperature

1 To make the cakes, position racks in the upper middle and lower middle of the oven, and preheat the oven to 350°F (325°F if using a convection oven). Line 2 baking sheets with parchment paper or nonstick liners.

2 Sift together the flour, cocoa powder, ground espresso, baking soda, and cinnamon.

3 Using an electric mixer fitted with the paddle attach-ment, beat the butter on medium speed for about 3 minutes, until soft and smooth. Add the sugar and salt and beat on medium high for about 5 minutes, until light and fluffy. Add the egg and vanilla and mix until blended. Scrape down the sides of the bowl. The mixture will look curdled, but trust me, it will all come together.

4 Add a third of the flour mixture and beat on low speed until just blended. Add half of the buttermilk and mix on low speed until just blended. Repeat with the second third of the flour mixture and the second half of the buttermilk, ending with the last third of the flour mixture, mixing until the dough just comes together.

FOR THE FILLING

4 ounces bittersweet chocolate, (preferably Valrhona Caraïbe 66%), finely chopped

2 tablespoons heavy cream

¾ cup (1½ sticks) plus 2 tablespoons unsalted butter, at room temperature

6 extra-large egg yolks, at room temperature

¾ cup confectioners' sugar

1½ teaspoons vanilla bean paste or pure vanilla extract

¼ teaspoon kosher salt

5 Using a 2-tablespoon ice cream scoop, shape the dough into balls and arrange about 2 inches apart on the prepared baking sheets. Bake for 10 to 12 minutes (8 to 10 minutes if using a convection oven), switching the baking sheets' positions halfway through baking, until the tops feel slightly firm and a toothpick inserted in the center of one cake comes out clean. Transfer the baking sheets to wire racks and let cool completely.

6 To make the filling, in a small heatproof bowl set over simmering water, heat the chocolate, cream, and 2 tablespoons of the butter until the chocolate and butter are melted. Set aside and save the simmering water.

7 Using an electric mixer fitted with the whisk attachment, beat the egg yolks on medium-high speed for about 3 minutes, until they become pale and thick. Add the chocolate mixture and beat on medium-high speed for 1 minute, until well blended. Place the bowl over the simmering water and cook the mixture, whisking constantly, for 3 minutes or until it is very thick.

8 Remove the bowl from the heat and set it in a bowl filled with ice and a little water. Stir occasionally until the mixture cools to room temperature. Add the remaining ¾ cup butter, the confectioners' sugar, vanilla, and salt to the cooled chocolate. Using an electric mixer fitted with the whisk attachment, beat on medium-high speed for 2 minutes, or until well blended and smooth.

(RECIPE CONTINUES)

Add some chopped-up Hazelnut Praline (page 210) to the filling of these whoopie pies. You won't be sorry you did.

9 Scrape the filling into a pastry bag fitted with a ½-inch plain tip. (You can use a 2-tablespoon ice cream scoop instead.) Arrange half the cooled cakes flat side up on a work surface. Pipe about 2 to 3 tablespoons of filling onto the center of each cake. Top with the remaining cakes, rounded side up, and press gently to push the filling to the edges. Store in an airtight container. The cakes are best eaten the same day they are filled but will keep for 2 to 3 days.

MAKES 45 Every time I make this recipe, it reminds me of nursery school recess and how the kids used to make fun of me for eating Fig Newtons. "Yucky," they would say when I pulled them out of my lunchbox. I loved 'em plain, and I loved mashing them in a bowl with soft vanilla ice cream. I should have realized at the time that my palate was just a tad different. These days, I love to eat these with Black Licorice Ice Cream (page 154). Swirl ⅓ cup of crumbled New T's into the finished ice cream for a simple dessert.

FOR THE FILLING

1½ cups (packed) trimmed and coarsely chopped dried figs

¾ cup red wine (preferably Merlot)

⅓ cup sugar

¾ teaspoon finely grated lemon zest

¾ teaspoon anise seeds

FOR THE DOUGH

½ cup (1 stick) unsalted butter, at room temperature

½ cup sugar

1 teaspoon vanilla bean paste or pure vanilla extract

1 teaspoon finely grated lemon zest

½ teaspoon kosher salt

1 extra-large egg, at room temperature

1½ cups all-purpose flour

1 To make the filling, in a medium saucepan, combine the figs, red wine, sugar, lemon zest, and anise seeds with 1 cup water. Cook over medium-high heat, stirring occasionally, until the mixture begins to boil, about 4 minutes. Once the mixture is boiling, reduce the heat to low and simmer, stirring occasionally, for 50 to 55 minutes or until the fruit is soft and the liquid is syrupy and reduced to about ½ cup. Set aside, stirring occasionally, until it cools to room temperature.

2 Scrape the cooled filling into a food processor and pulse until the mixture is smooth. Use immediately, or cover and refrigerate for up to 1 week.

3 To make the dough, using an electric mixer fitted with the paddle attachment, beat the butter on medium speed for about 3 minutes, until it is soft and smooth. Add the sugar, vanilla, lemon zest, and salt and beat on medium high for about 3 minutes, until well blended.

4 Add the egg and beat for 1 minute. Add the flour and beat on medium speed until just blended.

(RECIPE CONTINUES)

5 Arrange 2 large pieces of plastic wrap on a work surface. Divide the dough into 2 pieces, drop them onto the plastic, cover, and shape each into an even, flat disc. Refrigerate for about 1 hour, or until firm enough to roll out.

6 Put a large piece of parchment paper on a work surface. Working with one disc at a time, put the dough on the center of the paper and top with another sheet of parchment paper. Roll the dough into a rectangle slightly larger than 11¼ × 15 inches, stopping occasionally to peel away the paper, dust the dough lightly with flour, and reposition the paper so you don't get any wrinkles. Try to keep the rectangle shape nice and neat—this will help keep the cookie count accurate. Slide the dough in the parchment onto a baking sheet and refrigerate for 1 hour, or until the dough is very firm. If you want to chill it faster, put it in your freezer and chill for 20 minutes.

7 Position racks in the upper middle and lower middle of the oven, and preheat the oven to 350°F (325°F if using a convection oven). Line 2 baking sheets with parchment paper or nonstick liners.

8 Working with one sheet at a time, slide the dough onto a work surface and peel away the top piece of parchment paper. Dust the dough lightly with flour, and reposition the paper so you don't get any wrinkles. Flip over the dough and peel away the other piece of parchment paper. Using a ruler and a small knife, cut the dough lengthwise into 3 equal strips.

9 Scrape the fig filling into a pastry bag fitted with a ½-inch plain tip and pipe the filling down the center of each strip. Carefully fold the dough over the filling, and using your fingertips (there's not a lot of dough here), press to seal the edges together. Roll the cookie so the seam is on the bottom. Cut into 1½-inch-wide pieces and arrange them about 1 inch apart on the prepared baking sheets.

10 Bake for 15 to 17 minutes (12 to 15 minutes if using a convection oven), switching the baking sheets' positions halfway through baking, until the tops are pale golden and the bottoms are golden brown. Transfer the baking sheets to wire racks and let cool completely.

VARIATIONS

Apricot: Substitute the same amount of chopped dried apricots for the figs; substitute the same amount of finely grated orange zest for the lemon zest in the filling and in the dough; use white wine instead of red; and use poppy seeds instead of anise seeds.

Substitute dried cherries, cranberries, or golden raisins for some or all of the figs, and swap out any other flavor combination.

chocolate caramel peanut bars

MAKES 18 PIECES My assistant, Amy, has been working on perfecting the classic Snickers bar. Every new batch of caramel and peanut bars she makes comes closer to the real deal. No, let me rephrase: Amy's version transcends the store-bought ones, making her creation our most popular brunch item in the Hedy's Childhood Treats section of the menu at Michael's Genuine Food & Drink. Thanks for this one, Amers!

I make a double batch of these and store one in the freezer. I think they might even be better when served frozen. You decide.

8 ounces milk chocolate (preferably Valrhona), chopped

¾ cup sugar

⅓ cup heavy cream, at room temperature

6 ounces white chocolate (preferably Valrhona), chopped

1 teaspoon kosher salt

1 cup salted peanuts (preferably Virginia)

1 Line the bottom and sides of an 8½ × 4½-inch loaf pan with parchment paper or foil and grease it lightly (preferably with Pam). Melt the milk chocolate in a small heatproof bowl set over simmering water, stirring until the chocolate is melted and smooth. Remove the bowl from the heat. Pour half of the milk chocolate into the prepared loaf pan and spread it evenly. Freeze for 15 to 18 minutes, until cold.

2 Once the layer is cold, make the next layer. In a large saucepan, combine the sugar and ¼ cup water. Cook over low heat, stirring occasionally, until the sugar is dissolved and the liquid is clear.

3 Increase the heat to medium high and boil, without stirring, for 3 to 5 minutes, or until the sugar begins to turn golden brown on the edges. While gently and continually swirling the pan over the heat to even out the color, cook for 2 to 3 minutes, or until the sugar turns deep amber.

4 Slide the pan from the heat and slowly add the cream. Careful! It will splatter up, and the steam is hot. Stir until

(RECIPE CONTINUES)

FOR THE THIRD LAYER

6 ounces bittersweet chocolate (preferably Valrhona Caraïbe 66%), chopped

1 cup heavy cream

¼ cup natural dark cocoa powder (preferably Valrhona), for serving

Using an offset spatula, spread it evenly. Place plastic wrap directly onto the chocolate and press to smooth the top. Refrigerate for 1 to 2 hours or until very cold.

6 Once the second layer is cold, make the third layer. In a small heatproof bowl set over simmering water, melt the bittersweet chocolate. It's extremely important to keep the chocolate very warm over the water. Using an electric mixer fitted with the whisk attachment, beat the cream on medium-high speed until soft peaks hold when the beater is lifted. Add the very warm chocolate and beat on medium speed for about 1 minute, or until well blended and very thick.

7 Remove the plastic from the loaf pan and scrape the chocolate-and-whipped-cream mixture into the pan over the second layer. Using an offset spatula, spread it evenly. Place plastic wrap directly onto the chocolate and press to smooth the top. Wrap the whole loaf pan in plastic and refrigerate for 2 to 4 hours, or up to 2 to 3 days.

8 To serve, using the parchment paper or foil liner, transfer the candy to a work surface. Peel away the paper or foil, and place the candy on a cutting board. Sift the cocoa powder evenly over the top. Using a large knife dipped in hot water and wiped dry, trim off the edges. Cut the candy (dipping the knife in hot water and wiping dry between cuts) into ¾-inch-wide slices. Store in an airtight container in the refrigerator for 3 to 4 days.

fruit gelées

MAKES SIXTY-FOUR 1-INCH GELÉES Think of these as gummi bears on steroids. I love making these with local tropical fruits, like passion fruit, mango, and guava. These gelées really showcase their flavors in a straightforward way. Any unsweet- ~~~~ ~juice will work in this recipe, so be creative. You also might want to ~~~~ ~our favorite soft drink or cocktail. I really like bourbon and ~~~~ ~oni.

2½ cups sugar, plus more for dusting and serving

1 cup unsweetened fruit purée

2 (3-ounce) pouches liquid fruit pectin

I freeze extra fruit purée when the fruit is in season and abundant. There's nothing like having the bright taste of passion fruit all year long.

I like to coat the gelées with vanilla sugar, which I make by grinding dried vanilla beans (see note, page 148) with granulated sugar. There's no specific recipe for my vanilla sugar. Simply combine the two ingredients and keep covered until ready to use.

1 Line the bottom of an 8-inch square baking dish with parchment paper or plastic wrap.

2 In a medium saucepan, combine the sugar and the fruit purée. Cook over medium heat, stirring frequently, until the sugar is dissolved. Increase the heat to high and bring to a full rolling boil. Boil for 3 minutes. Remove from the heat and whisk in the pectin. Stir until well blended, and then pour into the prepared baking dish. Set aside at room temperature until completely cool and firm. The time will vary depending on the fruit used.

3 Run a small knife around the edge of the baking dish, invert the gelée onto a work surface, and peel off the parchment paper or plastic. Using a large knife, cut the gelée crosswise into eight 1-inch-wide strips. Cut each strip into eight squares. Store in an airtight container for up to 5 days.

4 Toss with extra sugar just before eating; otherwise leave the gelées alone until eating. The sugar melts if they are tossed too far ahead of time.

marshmallows

MAKES 40 (1½-INCH) MARSHMALLOWS What type of jet do they use to "jet-puff" those store-bought marshmallows, anyway? Homemade marshmallows are a revelation to those who have only had the supermarket varieties. While marshmallows remind me of sitting around a campfire at summer camp, my simple recipe is great year-round and for all occasions—without the need to figure out how to land a 747 in your kitchen for that "jet-puffed" effect.

⅓ cup cornstarch

⅓ cup confectioners' sugar

2½ tablespoons unflavored powdered gelatin

2 cups granulated sugar

1 teaspoon Lyle's Golden Syrup (found in most supermarkets)

2 extra-large egg whites, at room temperature

¾ teaspoon vanilla bean paste or pure vanilla extract

1 In a medium bowl, sift the cornstarch and confectioners' sugar and whisk together. Sift about a third of the mixture evenly over the bottom of a 9 × 13-inch baking dish.

2 In a small saucepan, sprinkle the gelatin over ¾ cup water and set aside for 3 minutes, or until the gelatin has softened and bloomed. Warm over low heat, stirring frequently, until the gelatin is dissolved and the liquid is clear (do not let it boil), about 2 minutes. Remove from the heat.

3 In a small saucepan, combine ¾ cup water with the granulated sugar and syrup. Cook over low heat, stirring occasionally, until the sugar is dissolved and the liquid is clear, about 3 to 5 minutes. Attach a candy thermometer to the side of the pan and increase the heat to medium high. Cook the syrup without stirring until it reaches 260°F, about 3 to 5 minutes.

4 Meanwhile—about when the sugar reaches 240°F—using an electric mixer fitted with the whisk attachment, beat the egg whites on medium-high speed until they form medium-soft peaks, about 2 minutes.

(RECIPE CONTINUES)

5 When the sugar syrup reaches 260°F, slide the pan from the heat and add the dissolved gelatin and the vanilla. Stir until blended.

6 With the mixer on medium-high speed, slowly pour the hot sugar syrup down the side of the bowl of egg whites. Continue beating the whites for about 6 minutes, or until the mixture cools and is only slightly warm.

7 Scrape the marshmallow into the prepared baking dish and spread it evenly. Do this step very quickly—the gelatin will cool fast and make it difficult to spread.

8 Sift another third of the cornstarch and confectioners' sugar mixture evenly over the top of the marshmallow. Set the dish aside at room temperature for about 4 hours, or until the marshmallow is very firm.

9 Run a small knife around the edge of the marshmallow and invert it onto a work surface. Using a large knife, cut the marshmallow crosswise into eight 1½-inch-wide strips. Cut each strip into 5 squares and toss with the remaining cornstarch and confectioners' sugar mixture. Store in an airtight container for up to 5 days.

VARIATIONS

Replace the vanilla with ½ teaspoon of one of the following pure extracts: coconut, almond, or maple.

Also, I like to add 3 tablespoons of cocoa nibs (see note, page 175) to the marshmallow right before removing it from the mixer. The little chocolate bites are delicious!

overstuffed nutters

MAKES 18 SANDWICH COOKIES My fascination with retro desserts began with my mom's love for the original peanut-shaped cookie of my childhood. She would have gladly passed up a meal for a cup of coffee and a plate of Nutter Butters.

I didn't mess with the recipe too much. I just combined two great recipes into one fantastic dessert: oatmeal raisin cookies (minus the raisins) and my favorite peanut butter cookie recipe. It's the same as the original, only better. You may call me cocky or foolish to think that I could improve on a classic, but you should try my cookies before you decide. I know my mom would think they're awesome.

FOR THE COOKIES

1 cup all-purpose flour

½ teaspoon baking soda

1 cup quick-cooking oatmeal

¼ cup chopped salted peanuts (preferably Virginia)

½ cup (1 stick) unsalted butter, at room temperature

½ cup (packed) dark brown sugar

½ cup granulated sugar

½ teaspoon kosher salt

½ cup creamy peanut butter (preferably organic), at room temperature

1 extra-large egg, at room temperature

1 teaspoon vanilla bean paste or pure vanilla extract

1 To make the cookies, position racks in the upper middle and lower middle of the oven, and preheat the oven to 375°F (350°F if using a convection oven). Line 2 baking sheets with parchment paper or nonstick liners.

2 In a large bowl, sift together the flour and baking soda. Add the oatmeal and peanuts and stir until well blended.

3 Using an electric mixer fitted with the paddle attachment, beat the butter on medium speed for about 3 minutes, until soft and smooth. Add the brown sugar, granulated sugar, and salt and beat on medium-high speed for 5 minutes, until light and fluffy. Scrape down the sides of the bowl. Add the peanut butter and beat for 30 seconds or until combined. Add the egg and vanilla and beat until just combined. Add the flour mixture, and beat on low speed until just combined. Do not overmix.

4 Using a 1-tablespoon ice cream scoop, shape the dough into balls and arrange them about 2 inches apart on the prepared baking sheets. Using the palm of your hand, flatten each mound slightly.

(RECIPE CONTINUES)

FOR THE FILLING

3 cups confectioners' sugar

10 tablespoons (1¼ sticks) unsalted butter, at room temperature

¾ cup creamy peanut butter (preferably organic), at room temperature

1¼ teaspoons vanilla bean paste or pure vanilla extract

½ teaspoon kosher salt

You can also try filling the cookies with the Mochaccino Whoopie Pies filling (page 26) or the vanilla filling for Overstuffed O's (page 47).

Try making ice cream sandwiches by baking larger cookies and filling them with Salted Caramel Ice Cream (page 149), Really Great Vanilla Ice Cream (page 146), or Buttered Popcorn Gelato (page 163).

5 Bake for 11 to 13 minutes (10 to 12 minutes if using a convection oven), switching the baking sheets' positions halfway through baking, until golden brown around the edges.

6 Transfer the baking sheets to wire racks and let cool completely. Store in an airtight container until ready to fill, or for up to 5 days.

7 To make the filling, using an electric mixer fitted with the paddle attachment, beat the confectioners' sugar, butter, peanut butter, vanilla, and salt on medium speed for about 3 minutes, until soft and smooth.

8 Scrape the filling onto a work surface and shape it into an 18-inch-long log. Cut the log into 1-inch pieces. Arrange half the cooled cookies bottom side up on a work surface. Put one piece of filling in the center of each cookie. Don't be afraid to overstuff these—the more filling the better. Top with the remaining cookies, top side up, and press gently to push the filling to the edge.

9 Store in an airtight container until ready to serve, or for up to 2 to 3 days.

overstuffed o's

MAKES 24 SANDWICH COOKIES Honestly, I've never connected to the Oreo experience. People love twisting off the top, licking the hydrogenated "cream," and eating the cookie. It finally clicked with me when I came up with this recipe, which takes the idea and makes it better by adding real chocolate, cocoa nibs, and fresh butter. These are little works of baked art.

FOR THE COOKIES

4 ounces bittersweet chocolate (preferably Valrhona Caraïbe 66%), chopped

1¾ cups all-purpose flour

⅓ cup finely ground cocoa nibs (see note, page 175)

¼ cup natural dark cocoa powder (preferably Valrhona)

1 tablespoon finely ground espresso beans

½ teaspoon baking soda

½ cup (1 stick) unsalted butter, at room temperature

½ cup (packed) dark brown sugar

⅓ cup granulated sugar

½ teaspoon kosher salt

1 extra-large egg, at room temperature

1 teaspoon vanilla bean paste or pure vanilla extract

¼ cup buttermilk, at room temperature

1 To make the cookies, melt the chocolate in a small heatproof bowl set over simmering water, stirring until the chocolate is melted and smooth, about 4 minutes. Remove the bowl from the heat and set aside to cool slightly.

2 Sift together the flour, cocoa nibs, cocoa powder, ground espresso beans, and baking soda. Make sure to toss any unsifted nibs back into the mixture.

3 Using an electric mixer fitted with the paddle attachment, beat the butter on medium speed for about 3 minutes, until soft and smooth. Add the brown sugar, granulated sugar, and salt and beat on medium-high speed for 5 minutes, until light and fluffy. Scrape down the sides of the bowl. Add the egg and vanilla and beat for 1 minute, until combined. The mixture will look curdled, but trust me, it will all come together.

4 Add the melted chocolate and beat on low speed for about 1 minute, until blended. Add half of the flour mixture and beat on low speed until just combined. Add the buttermilk and mix until blended. Add the remaining flour and mix until just combined. Do not overmix.

(RECIPE CONTINUES)

5 Arrange 2 large pieces of plastic wrap on a work surface. Divide the dough into 2 pieces, drop them onto the plastic, cover, and shape each into an even, flat disc. Refrigerate for about 1 hour, or until firm enough to roll out.

6 Position the oven racks in the upper middle and lower middle of the oven, and preheat the oven to 375°F (350°F if using a convection oven). Line 2 baking sheets with parchment paper or nonstick liners.

7 Put a large piece of parchment paper on a work surface. Working with one piece of dough at a time, put the dough on the center of the paper and top with another sheet of parchment paper. Roll the dough to a scant ¼-inch thickness, stopping occasionally to peel away the paper, dust the dough lightly with flour, and reposition the paper so you don't get any wrinkles. If the dough is too hard to roll, set it aside for 15 to 20 minutes until it is softer.

8 Using a round 2-inch cookie cutter, punch out rounds and arrange them about ¾ inch apart on the prepared baking sheets (they don't spread much, if at all). Reroll and cut the scraps once.

9 Bake for 8 to 10 minutes (7 to 9 minutes if using a convection oven), switching the baking sheets' positions halfway through baking. (If you like crisper cookies, add a minute or two to the baking time.) Transfer the baking sheets to wire racks and let cool completely.

10 To make the filling, using an electric mixer fitted with the paddle attachment, beat the butter on medium speed for about 3 minutes, until soft and smooth. Add the sugar, salt, and vanilla and beat on medium-high speed for 3 minutes, until smooth, light, and fluffy.

11 Scrape the filling into a pastry bag fitted with a ½-inch plain tip. (You can use a 2-tablespoon ice cream scoop instead.) Arrange half of the cooled cookies bottom side up on a work surface. Pipe about 2 tablespoons of filling in the center of each cookie. Top with the remaining cookies, top side up, and press gently to push the filling to the edges. Let the filling set so that it doesn't "splooge" out when you take a bite. Store in an airtight container for up to 2 days.

FOR THE FILLING

1 cup (2 sticks) unsalted butter, at room temperature

4 cups confectioners' sugar

1 teaspoon kosher salt

2 teaspoons vanilla bean paste or pure vanilla extract

VARIATIONS

Experiment with this recipe by playing around with different fillings; the chocolate filling of the Mochaccino Whoopie Pies (page 26) is killer. Adding crushed Hazelnut Praline (page 210) to the filling is awesome too. The cookies also make a great ice cream sandwich when paired with one of my recipes from the Everything Frozen chapter, such as Chocolate, Cherries + Chipotle Ice Cream (page 174); Coffee + Toffee Ice Cream (page 166); or Old-Fashioned Strawberry Buttermilk Ice Cream (page 152).

+ peanuts

MAKES 5 CUPS "Candy-coated popcorn, peanuts, and a prize. That's what you get in a Cracker Jack." I loved singing that jingle and eating the buttery, caramel-coated snack at Connie Mack Stadium with my dad, watching the Phillies play ball. Though I hated baseball, I loved the junk food. This is my rendition of that addictive summertime favorite snack. Do not attempt this recipe using microwave popcorn! Pop it old-school style for the very best flavor and texture. (Prizes not included.)

¾ cup sugar

1¼ cups salted peanuts (preferably Virginia)

Pinch of kosher salt

2 tablespoons (¼ stick) unsalted butter, at room temperature

3 cups freshly popped popcorn (recipe follows)

1 Line a baking sheet with a nonstick liner (parchment paper won't work for this). Grease the bottom of a metal spatula (preferably with Pam).

2 In a large saucepan, combine the sugar with 2 tablespoons of water. Cook over medium heat, stirring occasionally, until the sugar is dissolved and the liquid is clear.

3 Add the peanuts and salt, increase the heat to high, and cook, stirring constantly, until the sugar begins to turn amber at the edges. The sugar will look granular but will melt into a caramel. Continue cooking and stirring (to even out the color) for another 4 to 6 minutes, until the caramel is liquid and a deep amber.

4 Slide the pan from the heat and add the butter and the popcorn. Stir until the butter is melted and the popcorn is evenly coated with the caramel. Carefully and quickly pour the mixture onto the prepared baking sheet, and using the greased spatula, spread it into a thin layer. Reminder: This caramel stuff is freaking hot, so be careful!

(RECIPE CONTINUES)

5 Set the sheet aside at room temperature for about 1 hour, or until the mixture is completely cool and hard.

6 Break it into small clusters and store in an airtight container for up to 5 days.

popcorn MAKES ABOUT 5 CUPS

3 tablespoons canola oil
½ teaspoon kosher salt
¼ cup corn kernels
 (preferably organic)

1 In a 5- to 6-quart heavy pot, heat the oil and salt over medium-high heat. Add 1 or 2 kernels and cover the pot tightly. When these kernels pop, add the remaining kernels and cover the pot with the lid slightly ajar. Gently shake the pot, sliding it over the burner, until the popping slows to a few seconds between pops. This should take about 5 to 8 minutes.

2 Remove the pot from the heat and dump the popcorn onto a large cookie sheet. Make sure to fish out any unpopped kernels, or you will have large dental bills from your friends.

I love adding stuff to change the flavor of my Cracker Jacks. You can add spices such as chipotle chili powder, toasted cumin seeds, or sesame seeds to the caramel along with the popcorn. Or you can also sprinkle the hot mixture with smoked fleur de sel (you can find it online). No measurements for these additions are needed here. Just start with a pinch and see what you think.

brown bites

ies,
+ bars

bites

MAKES 36 PIECES These tropical bites pack in quite a lot of powerful flavors with the rich coconut and the crunchy, buttery macadamia nuts. Imagine pecan pie goes on a tropical vacation and comes home humming Bob Marley tunes.

Serve these alone or à la mode along with Rum Toffee Sauce (page 215) and Really Great Vanilla Ice Cream (page 146).

FOR THE CRUST

¾ cup (1½ sticks) unsalted butter, at room temperature

½ cup granulated sugar

Pinch of kosher salt

1 extra-large egg yolk, at room temperature

¼ teaspoon vanilla bean paste or pure vanilla extract

2⅓ cups cake flour, sifted

1 To make the crust, line the bottom and sides a 9 × 13-inch baking pan with parchment paper or foil and grease it lightly (preferably with Pam).

2 Using an electric mixer fitted with the paddle attachment, beat the butter on medium speed for about 3 minutes, until it is soft and smooth. Add the granulated sugar and salt and beat on medium-high speed for about 3 minutes. Add the egg yolk and vanilla and beat for 1 minute, or until well blended. Add the flour and beat on medium speed until just blended.

3 Scrape the dough into the prepared baking pan. Dip your fingers in flour and press the dough into an even layer to cover the bottom of the pan, redipping in flour as needed to keep things from being too sticky. Using the tines of a fork, prick the crust all over. Refrigerate for 15 minutes, until chilled.

4 Position a rack in the center of the oven and preheat the oven to 350°F (325°F if using a convection oven).

5 Bake for 20 to 22 minutes (18 to 20 minutes if using a convection oven), until the crust is pale golden. Transfer the baking pan to a wire rack to cool while you make the filling. Keep the oven set to 350°F (325°F if using a convection oven).

FOR THE FILLING

1 cup (2 sticks) unsalted butter, cut into 6 pieces

1 cup (packed) dark brown sugar

¼ cup granulated sugar

¾ cup honey (preferably organic and local)

1 pound macadamia nuts, coarsely chopped and toasted

½ cup sweetened shredded coconut

¼ cup heavy cream, at room temperature

½ teaspoon vanilla bean paste or pure vanilla extract

Pinch of kosher salt

6   To make the filling, in a large saucepan, melt the butter over low heat, stirring occasionally, about 2 minutes. Add the brown sugar, granulated sugar, and honey. Increase the heat to medium-high and cook, stirring occasionally, until the mixture begins to boil. Once the mixture is boiling, stop stirring and cook for 3 minutes.

7   Slide the pan from the heat, and add the macadamia nuts, coconut, cream, vanilla, and salt. Stir until combined. Pour the filling over the crust and spread it into an even layer.

8   Bake for 24 to 26 minutes (20 to 24 minutes if using a convection oven), until the filling is bubbling and deep brown. It will still look soft and very wet, but it will set up as it cools.

9   Transfer the baking dish to a wire rack and let cool completely (overnight is best).

10 To serve, use the foil or parchment liner to lift the cookie from the pan and onto a cutting board. Peel away the foil or paper, and using a large knife, cut the cookie lengthwise into 3 long strips, then cut each strip into 12 equal pieces. Store in an airtight container for up to 1 week.

s'more brownies

MAKES 12 BROWNIES The very first brownie I baked came from a packaged mix. I was six years old and couldn't wait to test out my Easy-Bake Oven. I carefully followed the directions step-by-step. I read and reread each line over and over again. I believed in the magic of that sixty-watt bulb that baked my brownie to fudgy perfection. In some ways, I'm still that six-year-old who believes anything is possible. This brownie is proof that magic happens, especially when you combine chocolate and homemade marshmallows and graham crackers.

8 ounces bittersweet chocolate (preferably Valrhona Caraïbe 66%), chopped

½ cup (1 stick) unsalted butter, cut into 6 pieces

¾ cup sugar

½ cup all-purpose flour

¼ teaspoon baking powder

½ teaspoon kosher salt

2 extra-large eggs, at room temperature

⅓ cup sour cream, at room temperature

2 teaspoons vanilla bean paste or pure vanilla extract

1 cup graham cracker pieces (preferably homemade; see page 85)

8 large marshmallows (preferably homemade; see page 41)

½ cup semisweet or bittersweet chocolate chips (preferably Valrhona)

1 Position a rack in the center of the oven, and preheat the oven to 350°F (325°F if using a convection oven). Line an 8-inch square baking dish with parchment or foil and grease it (preferable with Pam).

2 In a small heatproof bowl, melt the chocolate and butter over simmering water. Whisk until smooth, and set aside to cool slightly.

3 In a medium bowl, whisk together the sugar, flour, baking powder, and salt.

4 In a large bowl, whisk together the eggs, sour cream, and vanilla. Add the flour mixture and whisk well. Add the melted chocolate and stir until blended. Add the graham crackers, marshmallows, and chocolate chips and stir gently until well blended.

5 Scrape the batter into the prepared baking dish and spread it as evenly as you can (the graham pieces, marshmallows, and chocolate chips will make the top look lumpy). Bake for 24 to 26 minutes (18 to 19 minutes if using a convection oven), until puffed and the center still jiggles when the pan is gently shaken. (I think these brownies are at their best when slightly underbaked.)

6 Transfer the baking dish to a wire rack and let cool completely before refrigerating for 2 hours, or until cold and firm. Cut the cold brownie into 12 pieces and store in an airtight container in the refrigerator for up to 5 days.

peanut butter

fudge brownies.

MAKES 12 BROWNIES Back in the day, I made these for my Girl Scout troop. They were always a hit—and should have earned me a merit badge! I still love to whip up a batch to take to cookouts or parties.

8 ounces bittersweet chocolate (preferably Valrhona Caraïbe 66%), chopped

½ cup (1 stick) unsalted butter, at room temperature

¾ cup sugar

¼ cup all-purpose flour

¼ teaspoon baking powder

½ teaspoon kosher salt

2 extra-large eggs, at room temperature

⅓ cup sour cream, at room temperature

½ teaspoon vanilla bean paste or pure vanilla extract

⅓ cup plus 2 tablespoons creamy peanut butter (preferably organic), at room temperature

1 Position a rack in the center of the oven and preheat the oven to 350°F (325°F if using a convection oven). Line an 8-inch square baking dish with parchment paper or foil and grease it (preferably with Pam).

2 In a small heatproof bowl, melt the chocolate and butter over simmering water. Whisk until smooth and set aside to cool slightly.

3 In a medium bowl, combine the sugar, flour, baking powder, and salt and whisk until blended.

4 In a large bowl, whisk together the eggs, sour cream, and vanilla. Add the flour mixture and whisk well. Add the melted chocolate and butter and stir until blended. Add the 2 tablespoons of peanut butter and mix until combined.

5 Scrape the batter into the prepared baking dish and spread it evenly. Drop small blobs of the remaining ⅓ cup peanut butter evenly on top of the batter. Using a table knife, swirl the peanut butter into the brownie batter and then smooth the top.

6 Bake for 40 to 44 minutes (30 to 34 minutes if using a convection oven), until puffed and the center still jiggles

(RECIPE CONTINUES)

brownies, bites + bars   61

when the pan is gently shaken. (I think these brownies are at their best when slightly underbaked.)

7 Transfer the baking dish to a wire rack and let cool completely before refrigerating for 2 hours, or until cold and firm. Cut the cold brownie into 12 pieces and store in an airtight container in the refrigerator for up to 5 days.

FOR THE FILLING

⅓ cup whole natural almonds, lightly toasted

3 tablespoons sugar

¼ teaspoon ground cinnamon (preferably Saigon, see note, page 69)

¼ teaspoon ground ginger

⅓ cup coarsely chopped crystallized ginger (preferably Australian)

1 extra-large egg

1 tablespoon whole milk

3 tablespoons sugar

1 teaspoon ground cinnamon (preferably Saigon, see note, page 69)

⅔ cup seedless blackberry jam or Pop Jam (page 205)

5 In a small bowl, combine the egg and milk and mix with a fork until blended. Set aside this egg wash to put on the rugelach just before baking.

6 In a separate small bowl, combine the sugar and cinnamon and mix until blended.

7 Put a large piece of parchment paper on a work surface. Working with one disc at a time, put the dough on the center of the paper and top the dough with another sheet of parchment paper. Roll the dough into a 12-inch circle, stopping occasionally to peel away the paper, dust the dough lightly with flour, and reposition the paper so that you don't get any wrinkles.

8 Using a small offset spatula, spread half of the jam evenly over the dough, leaving a ½-inch border around the edge. Scatter half of the nut mixture evenly over the jam. Using your hands, press firmly on the nuts so that they stick. Using a chef's knife or a pizza wheel, cut the circle into 16 triangles.

9 Beginning with the wide end, roll up each triangle. They will look like mini croissants. Arrange the cookies, center tips tucked underneath, about 1 inch apart on one of the prepared baking sheets. Lightly brush the tops of the rugelach with the egg wash and sprinkle with the cinnamon sugar.

10 Bake for 35 to 38 minutes (30 to 35 minutes if using a convection oven), until browned. Transfer the baking sheet to a wire rack, and let the cookies cool completely.

(RECIPE CONTINUES)

11 While the first batch is baking, repeat the process with the remaining dough. The baked and cooled ruggies can be covered and stored at room temperature for up to 3 days.

VARIATIONS

Apricot, Cardamom + Pistachio: For the filling, substitute the same amount of ground cardamom for the ground ginger and the same amount of toasted pistachios for the toasted almonds. Substitute an equal amount of apricot jam for the blackberry.

Chocolate Chip, Cherry + Walnut: For the filling, substitute ⅓ cup lightly toasted walnuts, ¼ cup chopped chocolate, ¼ cup dried cherries, ¼ cup sugar, 1 teaspoon cocoa powder (preferably Valrhona), and ¼ teaspoon ground cinnamon and pulse in a food processor until finely chopped. Substitute an equal amount of cherry jam for the blackberry.

Saigon cinnamon contains the highest percentage of essential oil of all the varieties of ground cinnamon. It packs the most flavor, making this one the finest and most exotic of all cinnamon types.

salted peanut

brittle my way

MAKES 1 POUND I developed this brittle recipe as a result of the frustrations of making brittle in the high humidity of South Florida. It's not traditional by any means—you would never stir boiling caramel for fear it would crystallize and get sandy when it cools. My version doesn't get sticky, stays dry for weeks (if it lasts that long), and it won't stick to your teeth. I have a serious cult following for this brittle. Watch out, because before you know it, you'll be getting calls in the middle of the night for a brittle "fix."

1½ cups sugar

2 cups salted peanuts
  (preferably Virginia)

1 tablespoon fleur de sel
  or other coarse sea salt

1 Line a baking sheet with a nonstick liner (parchment paper won't work for brittle). Grease the bottom of an offset metal spatula (preferably with Pam).

2 In a large saucepan, combine the sugar and 1¼ cups water. Cook over low heat, stirring occasionally, until the sugar is dissolved and the liquid is clear. Increase the heat to medium high, and bring the liquid to a boil.

3 Add the peanuts and cook, stirring occasionally, until the liquid begins to turn light amber on the edges. (The liquid will look opaque, not clear like traditional brittles or caramel.) Continue cooking and stirring (to even out the color) for another 4 to 6 minutes, until the caramel is a deep amber.

4 Carefully and quickly pour the brittle onto the prepared baking sheet, and using the greased spatula, spread it into an even layer that is about ½ inch thick. Sprinkle with the fleur de sel. Reminder: This caramel stuff is hot, so be careful!

5 Set aside at room temperature for about 1 hour, or until the brittle is completely cool and hard. Break or cut the brittle into small or large pieces—depending on how hungry you are—and store in an airtight container for up to 5 days.

MAKES 24 BARS These guys are so unpretentious and easy to make that I hope they don't get overlooked by the experienced baker. They are a perfect vehicle to show off a prize-winning Pop Jam (page 205) or Grapefruit Marmalade (page 206).

Years ago, an assistant of mine shared with me her grandmother's technique of using a box grater to evenly distribute the dough. Unique, yes. Grating the dough gives these bars a light and airy texture. Careful with your knuckles, though!

3 cups all-purpose flour

1½ teaspoons baking powder

1½ teaspoons kosher salt

1½ cups (3 sticks) unsalted butter, at room temperature

1½ cups granulated sugar

2 teaspoons vanilla bean paste or pure vanilla extract

2 teaspoons finely grated lemon zest

3 extra-large egg yolks, at room temperature

1⅓ cups raspberry Pop Jam (page 205, or use really good store-bought)

⅓ cup confectioners' sugar, for dusting

1 To make the crust, sift together the flour, baking powder, and salt.

2 Using an electric mixer fitted with the paddle attachment, beat the butter on medium speed for about 3 minutes, until soft and smooth. Add the granulated sugar, vanilla, and lemon zest and beat on medium-high speed for about 2 minutes, until well blended. Add the egg yolks, one at a time, and beat for 1 minute or until well blended. Add the flour mixture and beat on medium speed until just blended.

3 Scrape the dough and any remaining floury bits onto a work surface and knead 3 to 4 times, until it all comes together into a smooth dough.

4 Divide the dough in half (weigh the halves if you have a scale), shape into logs, and wrap in plastic wrap. Freeze the logs for 2 hours, or until very firm.

5 Position a rack in the center of the oven, and preheat the oven to 350°F (325°F if using a convection oven). Line the bottom and sides of a 9-inch square baking pan with parchment paper or foil and grease it lightly (preferably with Pam).

(RECIPE CONTINUES)

6 Put a large box grater on a plate, and using the large holes, shred one of the logs (keep the other one frozen). Scatter the dough pieces evenly in the prepared baking pan, being careful to not press on the pieces. (You want the layers to be nice and fluffy.) Using a small offset spatula, spread the jam evenly over the dough without pressing down on the dough. Shred the remaining log and scatter the pieces evenly over the jam. The pan will be very full.

7 Bake for 54 to 56 minutes (40 to 45 minutes if using a convection oven), until the top is slightly puffed and evenly browned. Transfer the baking pan to a wire rack and let cool completely.

8 To serve, use the foil or parchment paper liner to lift the cookie from the pan and onto a cutting board. Peel away the foil or paper, and using a large knife, cut the cookie into 4 strips. Cut each strip into 6 equal pieces and dust with the confectioners' sugar. Store in an airtight container for up to 1 week.

Using a box grater to shred this dough is a great workout for your forearms. That said, if you're not into the workout, you can shred the dough in a food processor—just be sure to shape the dough into a long log that will fit into your processor's feeding tube. Also, be sure to work only with very frozen dough.

panforte

MAKES 36 PIECES A cross between fruitcake, candy, and honey cake, this is the Italian trifecta of desserts. Though panforte (pahn-FOR-teh) is often made in a circular pan and cut into wedges, I prefer to serve it as bars. You'll find that these taste better after they sit for a few days and the spices have had time to meld with the honey. Make this the new "fruitcake" for holiday gifts. It's much hipper and is delicious served with espresso or affogato, or alongside gelato.

2 (8-inch) squares rice paper

1½ cups all-purpose flour

¼ cup natural dark cocoa powder (preferably Valrhona)

1 teaspoon ground cinnamon (preferably Saigon, see note, page 69)

¼ teaspoon ground allspice

¼ teaspoon ground cloves

¼ teaspoon ground ginger

1 cup sugar

1 cup honey (preferably organic and local)

1 cup hazelnuts, toasted and coarsely chopped

1 cup whole natural almonds, toasted and coarsely chopped

1 cup (packed) coarsely chopped dried apricots

1 Position a rack in the center of the oven, and preheat the oven to 325°F (300°F if using a convection oven). Generously grease the sides of an 8-inch square baking pan (preferably with Pam). Line the bottom with 1 piece of rice paper.

2 In a medium bowl, sift together the flour, cocoa, cinnamon, allspice, cloves, and ginger.

3 In a large saucepan, combine the sugar and honey. Cook, stirring occasionally, over medium heat until the mixture begins to boil. Once the mixture is boiling, stop stirring and let cook until a candy thermometer registers 238°F to 240°F.

4 Slide the pan from the heat and add the flour mixture, hazelnuts, almonds, and apricots. Stir until well blended.

5 Working quickly, scrape the mixture into the prepared pan and spread it into an even layer. Top with the remaining piece of rice paper. Using an offset spatula, press firmly on the paper to make an even layer.

(RECIPE CONTINUES)

You can use any combination or type of dried fruit or nuts for this recipe. Dried figs, cherries, pistachios, cranberries, and pine nuts all make delicious panforte.

Edible rice paper can be purchased online.

6 Bake for 28 to 30 minutes (21 to 22 minutes if using a convection oven), until the filling is bubbling slightly on the edges. It will still look soft and very wet, but it will set up as it cools. Transfer the baking pan to a wire rack and let cool completely (overnight is best).

7 To serve, run a knife around the edge of the pan and invert onto a cutting board. Using a large knife, cut the panforte into 3 strips and cut each strip into 12 equal pieces. Store in an airtight container for up to 1 week.

cook

\+

ies
biscotti

eat dess... first

"hot chocolate" wedding cookies

MAKES 27 COOKIES Cinco de Mayo is my favorite holiday, and I celebrate it with passion. I worked for many years as a pastry chef at Mark's Place in North Miami. Mark Militello, the chef and owner, shared the same love of this holiday. Every May 4 and 5, we would transform the menu entirely to an authentic Mexican theme. The standout recipe for me was this amazing little cookie, which is jam-packed with flavor. My chocolate wedding cookies have a kick of spice and are so easy to make.

1¼ cups all-purpose flour

½ cup natural dark cocoa powder (preferably Valrhona)

1 teaspoon ground cinnamon (preferably Saigon, see note, page 69)

1 teaspoon finely ground espresso beans

½ teaspoon ground allspice

¼ teaspoon ground cloves

¼ teaspoon ground chipotle chili pepper

10 tablespoons (1¼ sticks) unsalted butter, at room temperature

¾ cup (packed) dark brown sugar

2 teaspoons finely grated orange zest

¾ teaspoon kosher salt

1 teaspoon vanilla bean paste or pure vanilla extract

Confectioners' sugar, for serving

1 Position racks in the upper middle and lower middle of the oven, and preheat the oven to 325°F (300°F if using a convection oven). Line 2 baking sheets with parchment paper or nonstick liners.

2 Sift together the flour, cocoa powder, cinnamon, ground espresso, allspice, cloves, and chipotle powder.

3 Using an electric mixer fitted with the paddle attachment, beat the butter on medium speed for about 3 minutes, until soft and smooth. Add the brown sugar, orange zest, and salt and beat on medium-high speed for about 5 minutes, until light and fluffy. Add the vanilla and mix until blended. Scrape down the sides of the bowl. Add the flour mixture and beat on low speed until the dough just comes together.

4 Using a 1-tablespoon ice cream scoop, shape the dough into balls and arrange them about 1½ inches apart on the prepared baking sheets. Bake for 14 to 16 minutes (8 to 10 minutes if using a convection oven), switching the baking sheets' positions halfway through baking,

until the tops feel slightly firm and the spices are very fragrant. Transfer the baking sheets to wire racks and let the cookies cool completely.

5 Store in an airtight container for up to 5 days. Dust with a little confectioners' sugar before serving.

Chipotle peppers are dried smoked jalapeños that have a wonderful earthy and smoky flavor with mild heat. The combination of orange, chilies, coffee, cinnamon, cloves, and cocoa is quintessentially Mexican. I love that so much flavor is packed into a tiny cookie.

trunk

MAKES 16 (2½-INCH) COOKIES Can a cookie define a career? Well, this is THAT cookie. Over the years, the recipe has remained basically the same—always gooey, salty, and amazing—with the supporting players changing depending on where my head is on a given day. I've added everything to this batter from peppermint patties to peanut brittle to peanut butter to stuffed pretzels. Be creative!

1¾ cups all-purpose flour

¾ teaspoon baking soda

½ cup (1 stick) unsalted butter, at room temperature

½ cup (packed) dark brown sugar

½ cup granulated sugar

¾ teaspoon kosher salt

1 extra-large egg, at room temperature

1 teaspoon vanilla bean paste or pure vanilla extract

6 ounces bittersweet chocolate (preferably Valrhona 70%), cut into ½-inch pieces

⅓ cup lightly crushed kettle-cooked potato chips

⅓ cup coarsely chopped salted pretzels

⅓ cup butterscotch morsels

12 malted milk balls, cut in half (about ⅓ cup)

⅓ cup salted peanuts (preferably Virginia), coarsely chopped

Coarse sea salt, for sprinkling

1 Sift together the flour and baking soda.

2 Using an electric mixer fitted with the paddle attachment, beat the butter on medium speed for about 3 minutes, until soft and smooth. Add the brown sugar, granulated sugar, and salt and beat on medium-high speed for 5 minutes, until light and fluffy. Scrape down the sides of the bowl.

3 Add the egg and vanilla and beat for 1 to 2 minutes, until just blended. Add the flour mixture and beat on low speed until just combined. Do not overmix.

4 Using a rubber spatula, scrape down the sides of the bowl. Add the chocolate, potato chips, pretzels, butterscotch morsels, malted milk balls, and peanuts. Stir until just blended. Don't be concerned if it seems like there is more junk than cookie dough.

5 Using a 3-tablespoon ice cream scoop, shape the dough into balls and arrange them close together on a large plate or small baking sheet.

6 Cover and refrigerate for at least 1 hour, until well chilled. The dough can also be covered and refrigerated

(RECIPE CONTINUES)

I bake these cookies just as customers enter the restaurant at lunchtime. The aroma fills the air and increases dessert sales. These are best eaten when fresh and warm, so have them the same day or promise you will reheat them just enough for the chocolate to ooze, giving them that just-baked feel.

Don't restrain yourself from tasting the dough. I love dropping mounds of this dough into ice cream as it's almost finished churning. Well, that's if there is any leftover dough. It makes great supercharged cookie dough ice cream.

overnight, or up to 2 days before baking. Reminder: Cold dough bakes better.

7 Position the oven racks in the upper middle and lower middle of the oven, and preheat the oven to 350°F (335°F if using a convection oven). Line 2 baking sheets with parchment paper or nonstick liners. Arrange the chilled dough balls about 2 inches apart on the prepared baking sheets. Using the palm of your hand, flatten each dough ball slightly. Sprinkle the tops with a little sea salt.

8 Bake for 11 to 13 minutes (8 to 9 minutes if using a convection oven), switching the baking sheets' positions halfway through baking, until light golden brown. I think these cookies are at their best when slightly underbaked and the chocolate looks oozy and gooey. Transfer the baking sheets to wire racks and let the cookies cool completely. Store in an airtight container for up to 5 days and reheat before serving.

cinnamon graham crackers

MAKES 30 COOKIES For those of you not familiar with this hurricane-prone, peninsula-shaped place referred to as the Sunshine State, key lime pie reigns supreme, and graham crackers play an important supporting role. (If you want to taste one of the best versions in Miami, just head over to Joe's Stone Crab.) Over the years, I have made many key lime desserts and have developed this great graham cracker recipe. Bake some of these babies, and I promise you won't buy store-bought grahams again. Yup, easy for me to say (I'm a pastry chef), but this recipe is super simple and delicious.

1¼ cups all-purpose flour

1 cup whole wheat flour

½ teaspoon baking powder

4 teaspoons ground cinnamon (preferably Saigon, see note, page 69)

½ teaspoon freshly grated nutmeg

Pinch of ground cloves

¾ cup (1½ sticks) unsalted butter, at room temperature

⅓ cup (packed) dark brown sugar

5 tablespoons granulated sugar

1 tablespoon honey (preferably organic and local)

1 tablespoon molasses

½ teaspoon kosher salt

1 extra-large egg, at room temperature

1 teaspoon vanilla bean paste or pure vanilla extract

1 Sift together the flours, baking powder, 2 teaspoons of the cinnamon, the nutmeg, and the cloves.

2 Using an electric mixer fitted with the paddle attachment, beat the butter on medium speed for about 3 minutes, until soft and smooth.

3 Add the brown sugar, 3 tablespoons of the granulated sugar, the honey, molasses, and salt and beat on medium-high speed for 5 minutes, until light and fluffy.

4 Scrape down the sides of the bowl. Add the egg and vanilla and beat for 2 minutes, until just blended.

5 Add the flour mixture and beat on low speed until just combined. Do not overmix.

6 Put a large piece of parchment paper on a work surface. Scrape the dough onto the center of the paper, and using your hands, shape it into a flat, even rectangle. Top the dough with a second piece of parchment paper. Roll the dough into a ¼-inch-thick rectangle that is slightly larger than 12 × 15 inches (about the same width

(RECIPE CONTINUES)

as the parchment), stopping occasionally to peel away the paper, dust the dough lightly with flour, and reposition the paper so you don't get any wrinkles. Try to keep the rectangular shape nice and neat—this will help you keep the cookie counts accurate.

7 Slide the dough in the parchment onto a baking sheet and refrigerate for 30 to 45 minutes, until the dough is firm. If you want to chill the dough faster, freeze for about 15 minutes.

8 Using a ruler and a small sharp knife or a pizza cutter, trim the dough into a perfect 12 × 15-inch rectangle. Cut the dough into 2 × 3-inch rectangles to make 30 cookies. I like to score the grahams just like the store-bought ones. Using the tines of a fork, prick the each rectangle twice—once at the top and again at the bottom—all the way through the dough.

9 Slide the parchment and dough back onto the baking sheet and refrigerate or freeze again for 20 to 40 minutes, or until the dough is very firm. The unbaked grahams can be stored in the freezer for up to 2 weeks (no need to thaw before proceeding with the recipe).

10 Position racks in the upper middle and lower middle of the oven, and preheat the oven to 325°F (300°F if using a convection oven). Line 2 baking sheets with parchment paper or nonstick liners.

11 Using a metal spatula, carefully lift the cookies from the parchment and arrange them about 1 inch apart on the prepared baking sheets (the grahams don't spread much).

You can bake all the scrap pieces of the dough and process them into graham cracker crumbs for later use.

I like dipping the grahams into melted chocolate and freezing them for a great midnight snack.

12 Mix the remaining 2 tablespoons sugar and 2 teaspoons cinnamon together and sprinkle evenly over the cookies. Bake for 22 to 24 minutes (20 to 23 minutes if using a convection oven), switching the baking sheets' positions halfway through baking, until the bottoms are golden brown. (If you like crisper cookies, bake for 3 minutes more.) You will start to smell them 15 minutes into the baking. The smell of cinnamon baking drives me insane.

13 Transfer the baking sheets to wire racks and let the grahams cool completely. Store in an airtight container for up to 3 days.

biscotti

MAKES 20 TO 24 BISCOTTI Working with sugar all day, every day, makes me realize how much sugar I consume on a daily basis, so I try to limit my intake. Having said that, anise biscotti are my weakness. These are simple, elegant, and straightforward. They combine my favorite flavors (anise notes, almonds), have a crunchy texture, and are not too sweet. Plain and simple, hands down, I love this biscotti.

1½ cups all-purpose flour

1 teaspoon baking powder

¼ teaspoon kosher salt

1 cup sugar

3 tablespoons whole anise seeds

1½ cups whole natural almonds

2 extra-large eggs, at room temperature

1 extra-large egg yolk, at room temperature

1 teaspoon vanilla bean paste or pure vanilla extract

1 Position a rack in the center of the oven, and preheat the oven to 325°F (300°F if using a convection oven). Line a baking sheet with parchment paper or a nonstick liner.

2 Sift together the flour, baking powder, and salt.

3 In a large mixing bowl, combine the sugar and anise seeds. Using your hands, rub the anise seeds into the sugar to release their oil. Add the flour mixture and almonds, and mix until well blended.

4 In a small bowl, stir together the eggs, egg yolk, and vanilla until well blended. Pour the egg mixture over the dry ingredients, and using your hands, mix well. The mixture will feel dry at first, and then it will come together to form a wet dough.

5 Scrape the dough onto the center of the prepared baking sheet. Using damp hands, shape the dough into a log about 14 inches long and 3 inches wide. Go ahead and rewet your hands if the dough gets sticky.

6 Bake for 33 to 35 minutes (30 minutes if using a convection oven), until the log is light brown and gives slightly when pressed. Do not overbake the log or you'll have trouble cutting it into neat slices.

7 Transfer the baking sheet to a wire rack and let cool until you can handle the log. (At this point, the biscotti can also be cooled completely, covered, and stored at room temperature for up to 1 day before proceeding.)

8 Reduce the oven temperature to 275°F (250°F if using a convection oven).

9 Carefully remove the log from the parchment paper or liner and place on a cutting board. Using a serrated knife and a sawing motion, cut the log on the diagonal into ½-inch-thick slices.

10 Line the baking sheet with a fresh sheet of parchment paper or nonstick liner.

11 Place the slices on the baking sheet, cut side down, leaving a little space between them. Bake for 15 to 18 minutes (12 to 15 minutes if using a convection oven), until they are dry. The second bake creates that great crunchy biscotti texture. To test for doneness, pull one out of the oven after 15 minutes and let it cool slightly. It should be very dry and firm at this point. If it feels right, pull the baking sheet out, set it on a wire rack, and let the biscotti cool completely.

12 Store the biscotti in an airtight container for up to 2 weeks. The longer they sit, the more the flavor develops.

VARIATION

Lemon-Pistachio Biscotti: Substitute the finely grated zest of 2 lemons (about 2 tablespoons) for the anise seeds and unsalted pistachio nuts for the almonds.

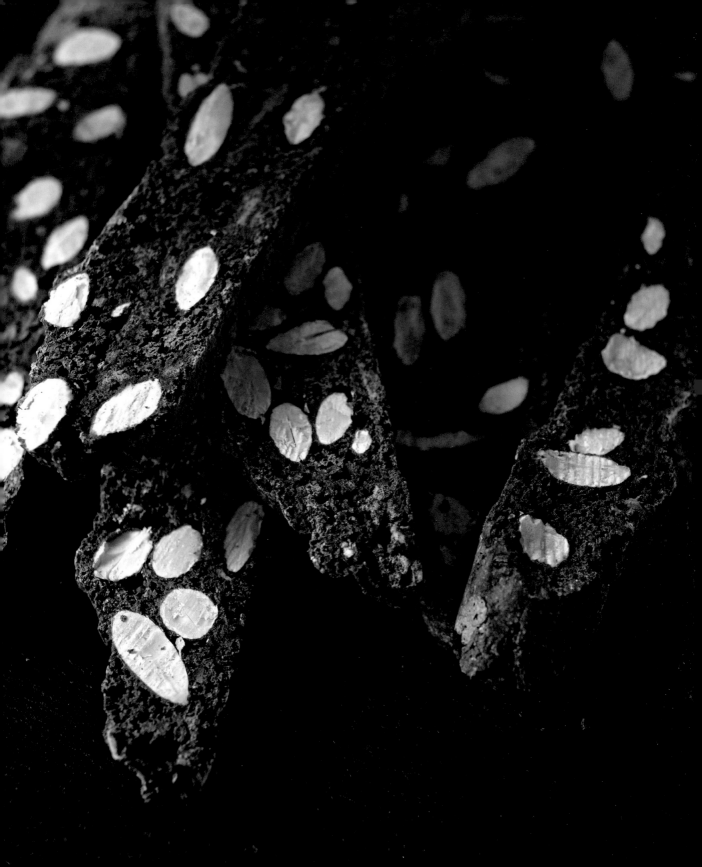

extreme chocolate biscotti

MAKES 20 TO 24 BISCOTTI I think of these as the rock stars of the cookie world. Simple to make and loaded with lots of big flavors, these biscotti taste even better the longer they sit . . . but they are so fantastic, they probably won't last very long.

1¼ cups all-purpose flour

¼ cup natural dark cocoa powder (preferably Valrhona)

1 teaspoon baking powder

¼ teaspoon kosher salt

1 cup sugar

2 tablespoons finely grated tangerine zest

1½ cups whole natural almonds

8 ounces bittersweet chocolate (preferably Valrhona Caraïbe 66%), chopped into ½-inch pieces

¼ cup cocoa nibs (see note, page 175)

2 extra-large eggs, at room temperature

1 extra-large egg yolk, at room temperature

2 teaspoons honey (preferably organic and local)

1 teaspoon vanilla bean paste or pure vanilla extract

1 Position a rack in the center of the oven, and preheat the oven to 325°F (300°F if using a convection oven). Line a baking sheet with parchment paper or a nonstick liner.

2 Sift together the flour, cocoa powder, baking powder, and salt.

3 In a large mixing bowl, combine the sugar and tangerine zest. Using your hands, rub the zest into the sugar to release the tangerine oil. Add the flour mixture, almonds, chocolate, and cocoa nibs. Mix until well blended.

4 In a small bowl, stir together the eggs, egg yolk, honey, and vanilla until well blended. Pour the egg mixture over the dry ingredients, and using your hands, mix well. The mixture will feel dry at first, and then it will come together to form a wet dough.

5 Scrape the dough onto the center of the prepared baking sheet. Using damp hands, shape it into a log about 14 inches long and 3 inches wide. Go ahead and rewet your hands if the dough gets sticky.

6 Bake for 36 to 38 minutes (30 to 34 minutes if using a convection oven), until the log gives slightly when pressed. Do not overbake the log or you'll have trouble cutting it into neat slices.

(RECIPE CONTINUES)

Here in Miami, the humidity tends to soften the biscotti, so before serving I throw them in the oven at a low temperature, about 250°F, for 5 minutes, just until they are dry. If your weather is similar, I suggest you do the same.

7 Move the baking sheet to a wire rack and let cool completely, about 2 hours. Don't be tempted to cut these while they are warm—the chocolate will ooze and the slices will be very crumbly. (At this point, the biscotti can also be covered and stored at room temperature for up to 1 day before proceeding.)

8 Reduce oven temperature to 275°F (250°F if using a convection oven).

9 Carefully remove the log from the parchment paper or liner and place on a cutting board. Using a serrated knife and a sawing motion, cut the log on the diagonal into ½-inch-thick slices.

10 Line the baking sheet with a fresh sheet of parchment paper or nonstick liner.

11 Place the slices on the baking sheet, cut side down, leaving a little space between them. Bake for 18 to 20 minutes (15 to 18 minutes if using a convection oven), until they are dry. The second bake creates that great crunchy biscotti texture. To test for doneness, pull one out of the oven after 18 minutes and let it cool slightly. It should be very dry and firm at this point. If it feels right, pull the baking sheet out, set it on a wire rack, and let the biscotti cool completely.

12 Store them in an airtight container for up to 2 weeks. The longer they sit, the more the flavor develops.

giant sesame

MAKES 12 COOKIES Growing up in Philadelphia and being Jewish meant eating Chinese food every Sunday night. We would eat the same boring things every week: wonton soup, egg rolls, spareribs (yup, love the pork), and fried rice. Dessert was always the best part: vanilla ice cream with many, many cellophane bags filled with fortune cookies. I couldn't resist ripping open that bag, breaking the fortune cookie in half, and getting to the fortune inside. The fact that paper was baked inside a cookie that was folded and at the same time crunchy was amazing to me. I've spent many hours trying to re-create that machine-produced cookie. I think I ended up with something that tastes so much better and is also really easy to make.

½ cup all-purpose flour

½ cup sugar

Pinch of kosher salt

⅛ teaspoon ground Szechuan peppercorns

2 extra-large egg whites, at room temperature

¼ teaspoon vanilla bean paste or pure vanilla extract

⅛ teaspoon toasted sesame oil

1½ tablespoons sesame seeds

 If you want to stuff fortunes inside the cookies, have the strips of paper ready before you bake the cookies. These cookies must be shaped while they are piping hot. They cool very quickly, so be prepared to work quickly.

1 Position a rack in the center of the oven and preheat the oven to 350°F (325°F if using a convection oven). Line several baking sheets with nonstick liners (parchment paper won't work for these cookies).

2 Sift together the flour, sugar, salt, and ground peppercorns.

3 In a medium mixing bowl, combine the egg whites, vanilla, and sesame oil and whisk for about 1 minute, until well blended and a little foamy. Add the flour mixture and whisk until smooth and well blended.

4 Spoon 2 teaspoons of the batter into mounds about 5 inches apart on the prepared baking sheets. I can fit 3 comfortably on my baking sheets. Using an offset metal spatula or the back of a wooden spoon, spread the batter evenly into 4½-inch rounds. Sprinkle with some of the sesame seeds.

5 Bake, one sheet at a time, for 9 to 11 minutes (5 to 6 minutes if using a convection oven), until the tops of the rounds are evenly golden brown.

(RECIPE CONTINUES)

6 Have a wide-mouthed glass or a coffee cup ready to help shape the cookies, along with a couple of baking pans (or rolling pins) standing by to help the completed cookies hold their shape while they are cooling. Working quickly, transfer the baking sheet to a wire rack. Carefully slide a metal spatula under a cookie and place the cookie upside down in the palm of your hand. (If the cookies are too hot to handle, use a work surface instead.) Put a fortune in the center and fold the cookie in half. Then, holding the cookie at each end with the opening facing up, bend the cookie until the ends almost touch. I like to bend the cookie over the rim of a wide-mouthed glass or measuring cup to help shape this last fold. Wedge the warm fortune cookies between the baking pans and let cool completely. Fold the remaining hot cookies. Don't expect perfection with your first cookie, but after a few tries you'll get the hang of it.

7 Repeat the spreading, baking, and folding with the remaining batter. Remember to use baking sheets that are completely cooled. Store in an airtight container for up to 1 week.

VARIATIONS
Substitute poppy seeds, anise seeds, lightly toasted black mustard seeds, or fennel seeds for the sesame seeds and omit the toasted sesame oil.

eat dessert first

rosemary shorts

MAKES 32 WEDGES A few years back, I was invited to dinner at my friend Debi's house. Deb is an amazing baker, and her kitchen is always loaded with beautiful jars of freshly made cookies and biscotti, so I wanted to bake something special to bring. These shortbreads rocked Debi's world, and she's been making them for cocktail parties ever since. They are awesome with a glass of pinot noir or a Super Tuscan.

2 cups cake flour

1 cup cornstarch

1 teaspoon baking powder

1 cup (2 sticks) unsalted butter, at room temperature

½ cup confectioners' sugar

3 tablespoons finely chopped fresh rosemary leaves

1 tablespoon honey (preferably organic and local)

1½ teaspoons kosher salt

1 tablespoon turbinado sugar

1 Sift together the cake flour, cornstarch, and baking powder.

2 Using an electric mixer fitted with the paddle attachment, beat the butter on medium speed for about 3 minutes, until soft and smooth. Add the confectioners' sugar, rosemary, honey, and salt and beat on medium-high speed for about 5 minutes, until light and fluffy.

3 Scrape down the sides of the bowl. Add the flour mixture and beat on low speed until the dough just begins to come together. The dough will be partially mixed, with a little flour on the bottom of the bowl.

4 Scrape the dough and any remaining floury bits onto a work surface and knead 6 or 7 times, until it comes together in a smooth dough. Do not overwork the dough or the cookies will be tough and crumbly. Divide the dough in half (weigh the halves if you have a scale), shape into flat discs, and wrap one disc in plastic wrap so it doesn't dry out.

5 Put a piece of parchment paper on a work surface. Put the unwrapped disc on the center of the paper and top it with a second sheet of parchment paper. Roll out the dough into a 9-inch round about ¼ inch thick, stopping

occasionally to peel away the paper, dust the dough lightly with flour, and reposition the paper so you don't get any wrinkles.

6 Peel away the top piece of parchment. Carefully position an inverted 9-inch cake pan or plate on top of the dough, and using a small sharp knife, trim around the edge to make a perfect 9-inch round. Using the tines of a fork, lightly press around the edge of the dough.

7 Cover the dough with plastic wrap and slide it, along with the parchment, onto a baking sheet and refrigerate for 30 to 40 minutes, or until the dough is very firm. If you want to chill it faster, freeze for about 15 minutes, until the dough is very firm. Repeat with the second disc.

8 Position the oven racks in the upper middle and lower middle of the oven, and preheat the oven to 300°F (275°F if using a convection oven).

9 Using a chef's knife, score each round into 16 equal triangles, cutting about halfway through the dough. Sprinkle the tops evenly with the turbinado sugar.

10 Bake for 30 minutes (22 to 27 minutes if using a convection oven), switching the baking sheets' positions halfway through baking. Shortbread cookies bake low and slow, so check to see if they have too much color. After 30 minutes (22 minutes if using a convection oven), you will start to smell the rosemary, and the tops of the cookies should be pale. If the cookies are browning too much, reduce the oven temperature to

(RECIPE CONTINUES)

275°F (250°F if using a convection oven). Bake for 10 to 12 minutes (8 to 10 minutes if using a convection oven) more, until the cookies are a very light tan color and feel mostly firm and dry.

11 Turn off the oven. Working with one baking sheet at a time, remove the sheet from the oven and place on a wire rack. Using a long straight-edged knife, carefully cut the round into 16 wedges, using the scored lines as a guide. The shorts need to be hot while cutting, or else they'll break apart.

12 Repeat with the other baking sheet and let the shorts cool completely. Store in an airtight container for up to 1 week.

VARIATIONS

Play around with using other types of herbs and spices. Black pepper and thyme are awesome in this cookie. You can also play with the salt amounts. Don't be afraid to add ¼ teaspoon more of salt and/or herbs to this recipe for a more savory taste.

These cookies are also great with Olive Oil Gelato (page 168) and Rhubarb-Blackberry Compote (page 209).

Extra-virgin olive oil may be substituted for the butter in this recipe; use 1 cup of the best olive oil you have. Eliminate the honey and increase the salt to 2 teaspoons. This will make a cookie that pairs great with a robust cheese.

mint chocolate

MAKES 32 COOKIES Many years ago, I was, in fact, a Girl Scout. Not just your average suburban variety, but a girl in a green sash with badges on a mission to sell the most cookies ever in the history of scouting. Thin Mints were my golden ticket to stardom—they made me the top seller in Philadelphia! No one can resist the rich dark chocolate shell and the crunchy, buttery, minty cookie hiding inside. If you think you love these Girl Scout cookies, just wait until you taste my version. They are stupid good.

1½ cups cake flour

½ cup cornstarch

½ teaspoon baking powder

¾ cup (1½ sticks) unsalted butter, at room temperature

½ cup confectioners' sugar

¾ teaspoon kosher salt

¼ teaspoon pure peppermint extract

1 teaspoon vanilla bean paste or pure vanilla extract

3 ounces bittersweet chocolate (preferably Valrhona 70%), finely chopped and chilled

1 tablespoon turbinado sugar

1 Sift together the flour, cornstarch, and baking powder.

2 Using an electric mixer fitted with the paddle attachment, beat the butter on medium speed for about 3 minutes, until soft and smooth. Add the sugar and salt and beat on medium-high speed for about 5 minutes, until light and fluffy. Add the peppermint and vanilla and mix until blended.

3 Scrape down the sides of the bowl. Add the flour mixture and the chilled chocolate (chilled chocolate keeps the dough nice and white) and beat on low speed until the dough just begins to come together. The dough will be partially mixed, with a little flour on the bottom of the bowl.

4 Scrape the dough and any remaining floury bits onto a work surface and knead 6 or 7 times, until it all comes together into a smooth dough. Do not overwork the dough or the cookies will be tough and crumbly. Divide the dough in half (weigh the halves if you have a scale), shape into flat discs, and wrap one disc in plastic wrap so it doesn't dry out.

(RECIPE CONTINUES)

5 Put a piece of parchment paper on a work surface. Put the unwrapped disc in the center of the paper and top with a second piece of parchment. Roll out the dough into an 8-inch round about ¼ inch thick, stopping occasionally to peel away the parchment paper, dust the dough lightly with flour, and reposition the paper so you don't get any wrinkles.

6 Peel away the top piece of parchment. Carefully position an inverted 9-inch cake pan or plate on top of the dough, and using a small sharp knife, trim around the edge to yield a perfect 9-inch round. Using the tines of a fork, lightly press around the edge of the dough.

7 Cover the dough with plastic wrap and slide the dough, along with the parchment, onto a baking sheet and refrigerate for 30 to 40 minutes, until the dough is very firm. If you want to chill it faster, freeze for about 15 minutes. Repeat with the second disc.

8 Position racks in the upper middle and lower middle of the oven, and preheat the oven to 300°F (275°F if using a convection oven).

9 Using a chef's knife, score each round into 16 equal triangles, cutting about halfway through the dough. Sprinkle the tops evenly with the turbinado sugar.

10 Bake for 30 to 32 minutes (20 to 21 minutes if using a convection oven), switching the baking sheets' positions halfway through baking, until the rounds are a very light tan color and feel mostly firm and dry.

11 Turn off the oven. Working with one baking sheet at a time, transfer the baking sheet to a wire rack. Using a

long straight-edged knife, carefully cut the round into 16 wedges, using the scored lines as a guide. The shorts need to be hot while cutting; otherwise they'll break apart. Repeat with the other baking sheet and let the shorts cool completely.

12 Store in an airtight container for up to 1 week. The flavor develops the longer they sit.

VARIATIONS

Toasted Cumin Shorts: Omit the peppermint and substitute 1 tablespoon lightly toasted cumin seeds for the chopped chocolate.

Anise Shorts: Substitute ½ teaspoon anise extract for the peppermint and 1 tablespoon lightly toasted anise seeds for the chopped chocolate.

custards,
+ pud

creams
dings

pots de crème

SERVES 6   The Orange Julius was a hit at the 1964 New York World's Fair. Who knew that orange juice, milk, and vanilla would be so delicious? It blew my mind as a kid, and I've been thinking of the perfect vehicle for the flavors ever since. This recipe is my homage to that amazing combo.

1½ cups heavy cream

1 vanilla bean, split (see note, page 107)

1 tablespoon finely grated tangerine zest

Pinch of kosher salt

6 extra-large egg yolks

½ cup sugar

½ cup fresh tangerine juice

1 Pour the heavy cream into a medium saucepan. Scrape all the seeds from the vanilla bean, and add them to the saucepan along with the bean, the tangerine zest, and salt. Cook over medium heat until very warm but not boiling, about 4 minutes.

2 Remove the pan from the heat, cover, and set aside for at least 30 minutes.

3 Position a rack in the center of the oven, and preheat the oven to 300°F (275°F if using a convection oven).

4 Arrange six 6-ounce ramekins in a baking pan that has 2-inch-high sides.

5 In a medium bowl, whisk the egg yolks and sugar until blended.

6 Over medium heat, bring the cream mixture back to barely a simmer. While whisking constantly, slowly pour the warm cream mixture into the yolk mixture until blended. Stir in the tangerine juice.

7 Pour the custard through a fine-mesh strainer into a clean bowl. Fish out the vanilla bean, scraping any remaining custard and seeds back into the mixture, and set it aside (see note, page 148). Discard the zest.

8 Pour the strained custard into the prepared ramekins. Put the baking dish into the oven, carefully fill the baking pan with very hot water to come halfway up the sides of the ramekins, and tightly cover the pan with foil.

9 Bake for 35 to 45 minutes (20 to 30 minutes if using a convection oven), or until the center of the custard jiggles slightly when a ramekin is gently shaken.

10 Transfer the baking pan to a wire rack, uncover, and let the pots de crème cool completely.

11 Remove the ramekins from the water bath and cover them with plastic wrap. Refrigerate for at least 8 hours, or up to 2 days. Serve chilled.

VARIATION

I like to make pots de crème with other citrus fruits, like Meyer lemons, grapefruit, or key limes. Feel free to substitute any of those here, adding up to 1 tablespoon of additional sugar to the recipe.

maple flan

SERVES 8 Miami loves flan, so I'm continually working on new recipes. This one is really delicious—not too sweet and so smooth and creamy. It's perfect any time of the year but makes a great holiday dessert wherever you happen to live.

3 cups heavy cream, at room temperature

¼ teaspoon kosher salt

1 vanilla bean, split (see note, facing page)

⅔ cup sugar

1 cup maple syrup (preferably Grade B dark amber)

7 extra-large egg yolks, at room temperature

1 In a medium saucepan, combine the heavy cream and the salt. Scrape all the seeds from the vanilla bean, and add them to the saucepan along with the bean. Cook over medium heat until just simmering, about 4 minutes. Remove the pan from the heat, cover, and set aside for at least 30 minutes.

2 Position an oven rack in the center of the oven, and preheat the oven to 300°F (275°F if using a convection oven).

3 Arrange eight 6-ounce ramekins in a baking dish that has 2-inch-high sides.

4 In a small saucepan, combine the sugar and 3 tablespoons water and cook over low heat, stirring occasionally, until the sugar is dissolved and the liquid is clear. Increase the heat to medium high, and boil, without stirring, for 3 to 5 minutes, or until the sugar begins to turn golden brown on the edges. Gently swirl the pan over the heat to even out the color and cook for 2 to 3 minutes longer, or until the sugar turns deep amber. Carefully and quickly pour the liquid evenly into the ramekins, swirling each one to cover the bottom completely.

5 In a large saucepan, bring the maple syrup to a boil over medium heat. Reduce the heat to medium low, and simmer for 8 to 10 minutes, or until reduced to ¾ cup. Keep an eye on the pot, and reduce the heat if the syrup threatens to boil over.

6　Slide the pan from the heat. Fish the vanilla bean out of the cream mixture and slowly add it to the pan. Whisk until blended.

7　In a medium bowl, whisk the egg yolks until blended. While whisking constantly, slowly pour the warm maple mixture into the egg yolks until blended.

8　Pour the custard through a fine-mesh strainer into a clean bowl.

9　Pour the custard into the prepared ramekins in their baking pan. Put the baking pan into the oven, and carefully fill it with very hot water to come halfway up the sides of the ramekins.

10　Tightly cover the pan with foil and bake for 45 to 55 minutes (25 to 35 minutes if using a convection oven), or until the center of the custard jiggles slightly when a ramekin is gently shaken.

11　Transfer the baking pan to a wire rack, uncover, and let the flans cool completely.

12　Remove the ramekins from the water bath and cover them with plastic wrap. Refrigerate for at least 8 hours, or up to 2 days.

13　To serve, run a thin knife around the edge of the custards and invert them onto small plates.

For the vanilla bean: using the tip of a knife, cut the bean lengthwise down the middle, leaving the top connected and the opposite end cut open.

key lime cheesecake flan

SERVES 6 Not a cheesecake, not quite a key lime pie, and not a traditional flan—what is it? A really good combination of everything Florida has to offer. I love to serve this flan topped with toasted Italian meringue (see page 133) and, if available, tropical fruits such as mango, lychees, or pineapple.

¾ cup sugar

4 ounces cream cheese, at room temperature

¼ teaspoon kosher salt

¾ cup evaporated milk, at room temperature

¾ cup sweetened condensed milk, at room temperature

2 extra-large eggs, at room temperature

3 extra-large egg yolks, at room temperature

1 teaspoon vanilla bean paste or pure vanilla extract

½ cup fresh key lime juice (from 14 to 16 key limes)

1 Position a rack in the center of the oven, and pre-heat the oven to 300°F (275°F if using a convection oven).

2 Arrange six 6-ounce ramekins in a baking pan that has 2-inch-high sides.

3 In a small saucepan, combine ½ cup of the sugar and 3 tablespoons water and cook over low heat, stirring occasionally, until the sugar is dissolved and the liquid is clear. Increase the heat to medium-high, and boil, without stirring, for 3 to 5 minutes, or until the sugar begins to turn golden brown on the edges. Gently swirl the pan over the heat to even out the color and cook for 1 to 2 minutes more, or until the sugar turns amber. Carefully and quickly pour the liquid evenly into the ramekins, swirling each one to cover the bottom completely.

4 Using an electric mixer fitted with the paddle attachment, beat the remaining ¼ cup sugar, the cream cheese, and the salt on medium speed for about 2 minutes, until smooth and fluffy.

5 Add the evaporated milk and condensed milk and scrape down the sides of the bowl. Mix on low speed until well blended.

6 Add the eggs, egg yolks, and vanilla and mix at low speed until just blended. Add the key lime juice and mix until incorporated.

7 Pour the custard through a fine-mesh strainer into a clean bowl.

8 Pour the strained custard into the prepared ramekins in their baking pan. Put the baking pan in the oven, and carefully fill it with very hot water to come halfway up the sides of the ramekins.

9 Tightly cover the pan with foil and bake for 35 to 45 minutes (20 to 30 minutes if using a convection oven), or until the center of the custard jiggles slightly when a ramekin is gently shaken.

10 Transfer the baking pan to a wire rack, uncover, and let the flans cool completely.

11 Remove the ramekins from the water bath and cover them with plastic wrap. Refrigerate for at least 8 hours, or up to 2 days.

12 To serve, run a thin knife around the edge of the custards and invert them onto small plates, scraping any liquid caramel from the ramekins onto the custards.

 Fresh juice is always the way to go, especially if you have access to great citrus. If you can't find fresh key limes, you can substitute regular (Persian) lime juice, Meyer lemon juice, passion fruit juice, or blood orange juice.

cinni mini bun pudding

SERVES 8 It's safe to say that I have baked hundreds of bread puddings in my career. It's a perfect way to turn leftover baked goods into something fantastic, completely transforming that day-old, less-than-fantastic stuff. Coffee cake pieces, corn muffins, croissants, doughnuts, and even Twinkies taste great. Cinni Mini Bun Bites (page 189) taste amazingly good in bread pudding—and look too cute. But don't hold your breath waiting for leftover Cinni Minis to make this. Make a batch of minis just for this recipe.

2 cups heavy cream

½ cup sugar

¼ teaspoon kosher salt

1 vanilla bean, split (see note, page 107)

1 tablespoon finely grated tangerine zest

4 extra-large egg yolks, at room temperature

½ recipe (about 18) Cinni Mini Bun Bites (page 189)

4 ounces cream cheese, cut into ½-inch pieces, at room temperature

1 In a medium saucepan, combine the heavy cream, ¼ cup of the sugar, and the salt, and stir to blend. Scrape all the seeds from the vanilla bean, and add them to the saucepan along with the bean and the zest. Cook over medium heat until just barely boiling, about 5 minutes.

2 Remove the pan from the heat and set aside for 15 minutes.

3 Fish out the vanilla bean, scrape any remaining custard and seeds back into the mixture, and set it aside (see note, page 148).

4 In a large bowl, whisk the egg yolks and the remaining ¼ cup of sugar until blended.

5 Over medium heat, bring the cream mixture back to a simmer. While whisking constantly, slowly pour it into the yolk mixture until blended. Toss in the Cinni Mini Bun Bites and stir to coat.

6 Set aside for 20 minutes, stirring occasionally, to allow the bites to absorb the custard. The bites should be soft and loaded with custard before baking.

(RECIPE CONTINUES)

7 Position a rack in the center of the oven, and preheat the oven to 350°F (325°F if using a convection oven). Lightly grease (preferably with Pam) an 8-cup baking dish (I use an 8 × 8 × 2-inch pan) or eight 1-cup ramekins and place it in a larger baking dish that has 2-inch-high sides.

8 Pour the custard mixture into the smaller baking dish and evenly distribute the cream cheese pieces over the top. Put the baking dishes in the oven and fill the larger baking dish with very hot water to come halfway up the sides of the inner dish.

9 Bake for 40 minutes (about 30 minutes if using rame-kins; 25 to 35 if using a convection oven) or until the top is light brown and the center of the pudding jiggles slightly when the dish is lightly shaken.

10 Transfer the baking dishes to a wire rack, and remove the inner dish from the hot water bath. Serve the bread pudding immediately, or allow it to cool completely and then refrigerate, covered, for up to 3 days.

If you don't like cream cheese, goat cheese and feta cheese also work well. The goat and feta cheeses add great saltiness to the bread pudding. Feel free to add chocolate chips, raisins, or any chopped dried fruit you like—about 1 cup total of stuff in addition to the cheese.

sweet corn +

SERVES 9 TO 12 Growing up in Philadelphia, my two favorite summer flavors were New Jersey–grown Silver Queen corn and fresh blueberries. I still remember the corn's sweet and buttery quality and those giant blueberries with their slightly tart snap and sweet finish. This is a great way to pair flavors that are not thought of together in a dessert.

   I wish I could share a brilliant story about how this recipe came to be, but it wasn't planned—it just happened. I had some leftover corn ice cream base, too little to churn and way too good to throw away. So I added cubes of brioche, fresh blueberries, and corn kernels to it, creating a new favorite summer dessert.

6 ears corn

2 cups heavy cream

2 cups half-and-half

1 cup granulated sugar

½ teaspoon kosher salt

2 vanilla beans, split (see note, page 107)

9 extra-large egg yolks

8 cups 1½-inch cubes of challah or brioche, crusts trimmed (day-old bread works best)

1 pint fresh blueberries, washed and dried

2 tablespoons turbinado sugar

1 Shuck the corn and peel away the silk. Holding the stem end of an ear, position the tip on a cutting board at a 45-degree angle. Using a sharp knife, cut away the kernels from stem to tip, rotating the ear and cutting until all kernels are removed. Repeat with the remaining ears. You'll end up with about 6 cups of kernels.

2 Put the kernels and the cobs in a large saucepan and add the cream, half-and-half, ⅔ cup of the sugar, and the salt. Scrape all the seeds from the vanilla beans, and add them to the saucepan along with the beans. Cook over medium-high heat until just barely boiling, about 5 minutes. Reduce the heat to low and simmer for 20 minutes.

3 Remove the pan from the heat and set aside for 15 minutes.

4 Using tongs, remove the cobs from the custard, scraping any remaining liquid back into the mixture, and toss them out. Fish out the vanilla beans, scraping any remaining custard and seeds back into the mixture, and set the beans aside (see note, page 148). Working in

(RECIPE CONTINUES)

I love this pudding after it chills and spends at least one day in the fridge. The texture is amazing when it's cold, but it's delicious either way.

Corn and blueberries go together so well, but, if you prefer, blackberries and huckleberries also work well. Use what is available and fresh.

batches, strain the mixture through a fine-mesh strainer set over a saucepan, firmly pressing on the kernels with the back of a spoon to extract every last bit of flavor and cream. You'll end up with about 4 cups of liquid; if it's less than that, add a touch more half-and-half.

5 In a large bowl, whisk the egg yolks and the remaining ⅓ cup of the sugar until blended.

6 Over medium heat, bring the cream mixture back to a simmer. While whisking constantly, slowly pour it into yolk mixture until blended.

7 Add the bread and blueberries and stir to coat the bread. Set aside for 20 minutes, stirring occasionally, to allow the bread to absorb the custard.

8 Position a rack in the center of the oven, and preheat the oven to 350°F (325°F if using a convection oven). Lightly grease (preferably with Pam) an 8-cup baking dish (I use an 8 × 8 × 2-inch pan) and place it in a larger baking dish that has 2-inch-high sides.

9 Pour the custard mixture into the smaller baking dish. Put the baking dishes into the oven and fill the larger baking dish with very hot water to come halfway up the sides of the inner dish. Sprinkle the turbinado sugar evenly over the top. Bake for 43 to 45 minutes, or until the top is light brown and the center of the pudding jiggles slightly when the dish is gently shaken.

10 Transfer both baking dishes to a wire rack. The bread pudding can be served immediately or cooled completely, covered, and refrigerated for up to 3 days.

bittersweet

SERVES 8 TO 10 Puddings are so easy to make. I have no idea why as a culture we buy the supermarket prepackaged, chemically enhanced, no-chocolate chocolate pudding for our families. Every time I make this one, I am blown away by the smooth texture and the in-your-face chocolate decadence. Homemade pudding is very simple to make, and oh so worth it. Serve topped with a spoonful of whipped cream if you'd like.

6 extra-large egg yolks, at room temperature

⅔ cup sugar

2 tablespoons natural dark cocoa powder (preferably Valrhona)

1½ cups whole milk

1½ cups heavy cream

¼ teaspoon kosher salt

8 ounces bittersweet chocolate (preferably Valrhona Caraibe 66%), chopped

2 tablespoons (¼ stick) unsalted butter, cut into 3 pieces and at room temperature

2 teaspoons vanilla bean paste or pure vanilla extract

1 In a medium bowl, whisk the egg yolks, sugar, and cocoa powder until blended.

2 In a medium saucepan, combine the milk, heavy cream, and salt and cook over medium heat until just boiling. While whisking constantly, slowly pour it into the yolk mixture until blended; then pour it all back into the saucepan.

3 Cook over medium-low heat, stirring constantly with a heatproof spatula—making sure you get the sides and bottom of the saucepan—until the pudding is thick enough to heavily coat the spatula and to hold a line drawn through it with your finger, about 3 to 5 minutes. The mixture will register 170°F on a candy thermometer.

4 Slide the pan from the heat, and add the chopped chocolate, butter, and vanilla. Stir until chocolate and butter are melted and the mixture is smooth.

5 Pour the pudding through a fine-mesh strainer into a clean 1-quart bowl. Press plastic wrap or buttered parchment paper directly onto the pudding surface to prevent a skin from forming, and refrigerate for at least 4 hours, or up to 2 days.

pumpkin streusel brioche bread pudding

SERVES 12 TO 16 When the holidays are coming and you're panicking trying to decide what to make for the in-laws (if not the Maple Flan, page 106), search no further than this recipe. This bread pudding will win over any fussy family member who insists on pumpkin pie. It's a large recipe—perfect for leftover care packages or late-night snacks. Serve it with the Bacon Maple Pecan Ice Cream (page 160), and you'll have a new family favorite.

This recipe is in loving memory of my dear friend Kay, who became one of my biggest fans and supporters. She was passionate about this bread pudding and dreamt about it all year long. She loved it, and I loved her.

FOR THE STREUSEL

1¾ cups cake flour, sifted

½ cup granulated sugar

½ cup (packed) dark brown sugar

½ cup chopped walnuts

1 teaspoon ground cinnamon (preferably Saigon, see note, page 69)

½ teaspoon kosher salt

10 tablespoons (1¼ sticks) unsalted butter, melted and cooled

1 To make the topping, in a medium bowl, combine the flour, sugars, walnuts, cinnamon, and salt and stir until blended. Add the cooled melted butter and stir until well blended. Refrigerate for at least 20 minutes, until the mixture is very cold and the pieces are about ¾-inch clumps. Keep refrigerated until ready to use.

2 To make the pudding, in a large saucepan, combine the heavy cream, half-and-half, sugar, ginger, tangerine zest, cinnamon, nutmeg, allspice, cloves, cardamom, and salt. Scrape all the seeds from the vanilla beans, and add them to the saucepan along with the beans. Cook over medium-high heat until just barely boiling and the sugar is dissolved, about 5 minutes.

3 Remove the pan from the heat, cover, and set aside for at least 30 minutes. Fish out the vanilla beans, scraping any remaining custard and seeds back into the mixture, and set them aside (see note, page 148).

FOR THE PUDDING

2 cups heavy cream

2 cups half-and-half

⅔ cup granulated sugar

3 tablespoons finely chopped fresh ginger

1 tablespoon finely grated tangerine zest

½ teaspoon ground cinnamon (preferably Saigon, see note, page 69)

½ teaspoon freshly grated nutmeg

¼ teaspoon ground allspice

¼ teaspoon ground cloves

¼ teaspoon ground cardamom

¼ teaspoon kosher salt

2 vanilla beans, split (see note, page 107)

9 extra-large egg yolks, at room temperature

1 (15-ounce) can pumpkin purée

2 tablespoons cognac or brandy

10 cups 1½-inch cubes of challah or brioche, crusts trimmed (day-old bread works best)

4 In a very large bowl, whisk together the egg yolks, pumpkin purée, and cognac.

5 Over medium heat, bring the cream mixture back to a simmer. Whisking constantly, slowly pour it into the yolk mixture until blended. Add the bread and stir to coat.

6 Set aside for 20 minutes, stirring occasionally, to allow the bread to absorb the custard.

7 Position an oven rack in the center of the oven, and preheat the oven to 350°F (325°F if using a convection oven). Lightly grease (preferably with Pam) a 12-cup baking dish (I use a 9 × 13-inch pan) and place it in a larger baking pan that has 2-inch-high sides.

8 Pour the custard mixture into the smaller baking dish. Put the baking dishes into the oven and carefully fill the larger baking dish with very hot water to come halfway up the sides of the inner dish. Bake for 20 minutes (15 minutes if using a convection oven).

9 Remove the pans from the oven and scatter the streusel evenly over the top of the custard. Bake for another 35 to 40 minutes (20 to 25 minutes if using a convection oven), or until the topping is golden brown and the center of the pudding jiggles slightly when the dish is gently shaken.

10 Transfer the baking dishes to a wire rack, and remove the inner dish from the hot water bath. Serve the bread pudding immediately, or allow it to cool completely and then refrigerate, covered, for up to 3 days.

panna cotta

SERVES 6 Nothing compares to the aromatic experience that fresh herbs deliver. While this recipe is great all by itself, without any herbs, it's spectacular with basil, which I keep calling the new mint. Michael Schwartz, the owner and chef of Michael's Genuine Food & Drink, loves this panna cotta. It speaks to his philosophy of straightforward flavors. Start with excellent ingredients, keep it simple, and you will have an awesome outcome.

1 cup heavy cream, at room temperature

1 vanilla bean, split (see note, page 107)

½ cup sugar

1 cup (packed) fresh basil leaves, washed and dried

1 tablespoon finely grated lemon zest

Pinch of kosher salt

1¼ teaspoons unflavored powdered gelatin

1½ cups buttermilk, at room temperature

1½ cups mixed fresh berries, washed and dried, for serving

Strawberry Consommé (page 201), for serving (optional)

1 Pour the heavy cream into a medium saucepan. Scrape all the seeds from the vanilla bean, and add them to the saucepan along with the bean, sugar, basil, lemon zest, and salt. Cook over medium heat until just boiling, about 5 minutes.

2 Remove the pan from the heat, cover, and set aside for at least 30 minutes.

3 In a small bowl, sprinkle the gelatin over 4 teaspoons of water and set aside to soften and bloom.

4 Fish out the vanilla bean, scraping any remaining custard and seeds back into the mixture, and set it aside (see note, page 148).

5 Over medium heat, bring the cream mixture back to just barely a simmer.

6 Slide the pan from the heat, add the softened gelatin, and stir until dissolved.

7 Pour the custard through a fine-mesh strainer into a clean bowl, pressing on the basil and the zest to make sure you get all of the flavor from them. Discard the basil and the zest.

8 Add the buttermilk to the cream mixture, and stir until well blended.

9 Pour the custard into 6 small straight-sided rocks glasses (about 6 ounces each, the kind you would use for a good bourbon). Cover the glasses with plastic wrap and refrigerate for at least 8 hours, or up to 2 days.

10 To serve, spoon the berries on top of the panna cotta and pour some of the Strawberry Consommé over the fruit, if desired. The consommé adds a pop of color as well as a great berry flavor.

pies,

+

FOR THE FILLING

2¼ cups coconut milk

¼ teaspoon kosher salt

1 vanilla bean, split (see note, page 107)

1 cup shredded unsweetened coconut

1¼ teaspoons unflavored powdered gelatin

3 tablespoons dark rum

6 extra-large egg yolks, at room temperature

½ cup granulated sugar

5 Position a rack in the middle of the oven, and preheat the oven to 375°F (350°F if using a convection oven).

6 Line the chilled crust with foil and fill with dried beans to weight it down. Bake for 25 minutes or until the edges are light brown and the crust looks dry. Carefully lift out the foil and beans, and continue to bake for 2 to 5 minutes longer, or until the crust is golden brown. Transfer to a wire rack to cool completely.

7 To make the filling, in a medium saucepan, combine the coconut milk and salt. Scrape the seeds from the vanilla bean, and add the seeds and bean to the pan along with the shredded coconut. Cook over medium heat until just barely boiling, about 5 minutes. Remove from the heat, cover, and set aside for at least 30 minutes.

8 In a small ramekin, sprinkle the gelatin over the rum and set aside to soften and bloom.

9 In a medium bowl, whisk together the egg yolks and sugar.

10 Over medium heat, bring the coconut milk mixture back to a simmer. While whisking constantly, slowly pour it into the yolk mixture until blended; then pour it all back into the pan. Cook over medium-low heat, stirring constantly with a heatproof spatula—making sure you get the sides and bottom of the saucepan—until the custard is thick enough to heavily coat the spatula and to hold a line drawn through it with your finger, 3 to 5 minutes.

11 Slide the pan from the heat, add the softened gelatin, and stir until dissolved.

12 Pour the custard through a fine-mesh strainer into a bowl, firmly pressing on the coconut with the back of a spoon. Fish out the vanilla bean, scrape any remaining milk and seeds back into the milk, and set the bean aside (see note, page 148). Rinse the coconut, spread it over paper towels, and set aside to dry.

13 Pour the strained custard into the baked pie shell. Press plastic wrap or buttered parchment paper directly onto the custard surface to prevent a skin from forming, and refrigerate for at least 4 hours, or up to 1 day.

14 To make the topping, position an oven rack in the middle of the oven, and preheat the oven to 350°F (325°F if using a convection oven).

15 Spread the coconut in an even layer on a baking sheet. Bake, stirring occasionally, for 8 to 10 minutes (7 to 8 minutes if using a convection oven), or until evenly browned.

16 Transfer the baking sheet to a wire rack and let the coconut cool completely. Use immediately or store in an airtight container for up to 1 day.

17 Using an electric mixer fitted with the whisk attachment, whip the heavy cream, crème fraîche, and sugar on medium-high speed for 3 to 5 minutes, or until the cream holds medium-firm peaks when the beater is lifted. Be careful not to overwhip the cream.

18 Spread the whipped cream over the chilled filling and sprinkle with the toasted coconut. Serve immediately or refrigerate for up to 1 hour.

FOR THE TOPPING

1 cup shredded unsweetened coconut

1 cup heavy cream

2 tablespoons crème fraîche

1 tablespoon confectioners' sugar

lemon meringue

SERVES 10 TO 12 Pairing tart lemon curd with sweet Italian meringue is a no-brainer. Opposites attract. They are heavenly when eaten together and combine to make the perfect dessert. This is not your run-of-the-mill typical diner-style lemon meringue pie. It's lighter than air, and the butter makes it as smooth as silk. The Italian meringue is rich and indulgent, yet so simple to whip up. I like making and serving this dessert as a whole pie. If you prefer, you can make individual tartlets, using 4-inch tart pans. This tart is wonderful with Rhubarb-Blackberry Compote (page 209).

FOR THE CRUST

1½ cups all-purpose flour

2 tablespoons sugar

½ teaspoon kosher salt

½ cup (1 stick) unsalted butter, cut into small cubes and very cold

3 tablespoons ice-cold water

1 To make the crust, using an electric mixer fitted with the paddle attachment, mix the flour, sugar, and salt on medium speed for about 1 minute, until blended. Add the butter and mix on medium-low speed for about 3 minutes, or until the largest pieces are about pea size. With the mixer on medium speed, add the water and beat for 1 minute, or until the dough forms moist clumps. Scrape the dough and any remaining floury bits onto a work surface and knead 3 to 4 times, until it all comes together into a smooth dough. Shape into a disc, wrap in plastic wrap, and refrigerate for about 1 hour, or until firm enough to roll out.

2 Put a large piece of parchment paper (or two taped together) on a work surface. Put the dough in the center of the paper and top with a second piece of parchment (or two taped together). Roll out the dough into a 14-inch circle, stopping occasionally to peel away the paper, dust the dough lightly with flour, and reposition the paper so you don't get any wrinkles.

3 Roll the dough loosely around the rolling pin and center it over a 10-inch springform pan. Unroll the dough evenly into the pan. Using your fingers, gently press the

(RECIPE CONTINUES)

FOR THE FILLING

1½ cups sugar

6 tablespoons finely grated lemon zest

8 extra-large eggs, at room temperature

1¼ cups fresh lemon juice

Big pinch of kosher salt

1¼ cups (3½ sticks) unsalted butter, cut into 2-inch pieces and at room temperature

dough onto the sides and bottom of the pan. Trim off all but 2 inches of the dough that hangs off the edge of the pan. Refrigerate for 1 hour, or until the dough is very firm.

4 Position a rack in the middle of the oven, and preheat the oven to 375°F (350°F if using a convection oven).

5 Line the chilled crust with a large piece of foil and fill it with dried beans to weight it down. Bake for 35 minutes (23 to 25 minutes if using convection), or until the edges are light brown and the dough looks dry. Carefully lift out the foil and beans and bake for 3 to 5 minutes (1 to 2 minutes if using convection) or until the crust is golden brown. Transfer to a wire rack and let cool completely.

6 To make the filling, in a large heatproof bowl, combine the sugar and lemon zest. Using your hands, rub the zest into the sugar to release its oil. Add the eggs, lemon juice, and salt and whisk until well blended.

7 Set the bowl over simmering water. Cook, whisking constantly, for 25 to 30 minutes, or until the mixture is very thick. Remove from the heat and pour the mixture through a fine-mesh strainer into a clean bowl. Set the mixture aside and whisk occasionally until it cools slightly, about 5 minutes.

8 Pour the mixture into a blender (if you have a small one, do this in batches). Partially cover the blender with the lid, and with the blender on low, add the butter, piece by piece, until the mixture is smooth and blended. Cover the blender completely, increase the speed to high, and blend for 5 minutes.

9 Pour the filling into the baked tart crust (if blending in batches, whisk them together before pouring into the crust). Cover the pan and refrigerate for 4 to 6 hours, until the filling is firm, or for up to 2 days.

10 To make the meringue, in a small saucepan, combine the sugar and ⅓ cup water and cook over low heat, stirring occasionally, until the sugar is dissolved and the liquid is clear. Attach a candy thermometer to the side of the pan and increase the heat to medium high.

11 When the sugar reaches 220°F, using an electric mixer fitted with the whisk attachment, whip the egg whites on medium-high speed until they form medium-soft peaks.

12 When the sugar syrup reaches 240°F, after about 5 minutes, slide the pan from the heat. With the mixer on medium-high speed, slowly pour the hot sugar syrup down the side of the bowl. Continue whipping the whites for 5 minutes or until the mixture cools to slightly warm and is stiff and shiny.

13 Pile the meringue on the chilled pie, and using a metal spatula, spread it over the filling. Serve immediately, or refrigerate, uncovered, for up to 8 hours.

14 To serve, remove the outer ring of the pan, and using 2 large offset spatulas, move the tart to a flat serving plate. Using a large knife dipped in hot water and wiped dry, cut the tart into slices, dipping the knife in hot water and wiping dry in between cuts. The tart is best if eaten the same day, but it will taste great the next day too.

FOR THE MERINGUE
¾ cup sugar
4 extra-large egg whites,
   at room temperature

If you have a handheld kitchen torch, use it to toast the top of the meringue evenly before slicing. If not, the pie is perfect without toasting. Do not put the pie under the broiler to toast; the butter that makes the filling so delicious cannot stand up to the heat.

fudge tart

SERVES 10 TO 12 Every baker needs an awesome chocolate tart that's easy to make and really fabulous. I think this recipe hits all levels. It's like a super rich brownie-like "mud" tart. Serve it with Chocolate, Cherries + Chipotle Ice Cream (page 174).

FOR THE CRUST

1½ cups all-purpose flour

2 tablespoons sugar

½ teaspoon kosher salt

½ cup (1 stick) unsalted butter, cut into small cubes and very cold

3 tablespoons ice-cold water

FOR THE FILLING

2 ounces semisweet chocolate (preferably Valrhona), chopped

1 cup (2 sticks) unsalted butter, cut into 2-inch pieces

½ cup natural dark cocoa powder (preferably Valrhona)

1½ cups sugar

3 tablespoons Lyle's Golden Syrup

3 tablespoons sour cream

4 extra-large eggs, at room temperature

1 extra-large egg yolk, at room temperature

¼ cup bourbon (preferably Maker's Mark)

1 teaspoon vanilla bean paste or pure vanilla extract

¼ teaspoon kosher salt

1 To make the crust, using an electric mixer fitted with the paddle attachment, mix the flour, sugar, and salt on medium speed for about 1 minute, until blended. Add the cold butter pieces and mix on medium-low speed for about 3 minutes, or until the largest pieces of butter are about pea size. With the mixer on medium speed, add the cold water and beat for 1 minute, or until the dough forms moist clumps.

2 Scrape the dough and any remaining floury bits onto a work surface and knead 3 to 4 times, until it all comes together into a smooth dough. Shape into a disc, wrap in plastic wrap, and refrigerate for about 1 hour, or until firm enough to roll out.

3 Put a large piece of parchment paper (or two taped together) on a work surface. Put the dough in the center of the paper and top with a second sheet of parchment paper (or two taped together). Roll out the dough into a 14-inch circle, stopping occasionally to peel away the paper, dust the dough lightly with flour, and reposition the paper so you don't get any wrinkles.

4 Roll the dough loosely around the rolling pin and center it over a 10-inch springform pan. Unroll the dough evenly into the pan. Using your fingers, gently press the dough into the sides and bottom of the pan. Trim off all but 2 inches of dough that hangs off the sides of the pan. Refrigerate for 1 hour, or until the dough is very firm.

(RECIPE CONTINUES)

Maker's Mark is always my go-to bourbon when baking chocolate desserts. Knob Creek runs a close second, and I love sipping Pappy Van Winkle while the tart is in the oven.

5 Position a rack in the middle of the oven and preheat the oven to 375°F (350°F if using a convection oven).

6 Line the chilled crust with a large piece of foil and fill it with dried beans to weight it down. Bake for 35 minutes (15 to 20 minutes if using a convection oven), or until the edges are light brown and the dough looks dry. Carefully lift out the foil and beans and continue to bake for 3 to 5 minutes (1 to 2 minutes if using a convection oven) longer, or until the crust is golden brown.

7 To make the filling, reduce the oven temperature to 325°F (300°F if using a convection oven).

8 In a large heatproof bowl, melt the chocolate and butter over simmering water.

9 Remove the bowl from the heat, add the cocoa, and whisk until blended. Add the sugar, Lyle's Golden Syrup, and sour cream and whisk until blended. Add the eggs, egg yolk, bourbon, vanilla, and salt and whisk just until blended. Pour into the baked tart shell.

10 Bake for 40 to 42 minutes (30 to 35 minutes if using a convection oven), or until the edges are slightly puffed and the center of the filling jiggles slightly when the pan is gently shaken. Transfer the pan to a wire rack and let cool completely. Cover and refrigerate overnight, or for up to 3 days.

11 To serve, unclasp and remove the outer ring of the pan, and using 2 large offset spatulas, move the tart to a flat serving plate. Using a large knife dipped in hot water and wiped dry, cut the tart into slices, dipping the knife in hot water and wiping dry in between cuts.

SERVES 10 TO 12 Simple yet elegant, rustic but dynamic, crostatas are a wonderful way to showcase two of summer's best fruits: peaches and blueberries. This free-form crust is filled with a ground nut–butter mixture and then topped with fruit. For the crust, I like to use a sauvignon blanc or dry chardonnay. Choose one you'd like to sip while the dough is "chillin'."

FOR THE CRUST

2 cups all-purpose flour

¼ cup granulated sugar

2 tablespoons yellow cornmeal

1 tablespoon finely grated lemon zest

1½ teaspoons kosher salt

¾ cup (1½ sticks) unsalted butter, cut into small cubes and very cold

¼ cup cold dry white wine

FOR THE FRANGIPANE

½ cup finely ground toasted almonds or hazelnuts

¼ cup (½ stick) unsalted butter, at room temperature

¼ cup granulated sugar

1 tablespoon finely grated lemon zest

Pinch of kosher salt

1 extra-large egg, at room temperature

2 tablespoons all-purpose flour

1 To make the crust, using an electric mixer fitted with the paddle attachment, mix the flour, sugar, cornmeal, lemon zest, and salt on medium speed for about 1 minute, until blended. Add the cold butter pieces and mix on medium-low speed for about 3 minutes, or until the largest pieces of butter are about pea size. With the mixer on medium speed, add the wine and beat for 1 minute, or until the dough forms moist clumps.

2 Scrape the dough and any remaining floury bits onto a work surface and knead 3 to 4 times, until it all comes together into a smooth dough. Shape into a disc, wrap in plastic wrap, and refrigerate for about 1 hour, or until firm enough to roll out.

3 Meanwhile, make the frangipane. Using an electric mixer fitted with the paddle attachment, beat the ground nuts, butter, sugar, lemon zest, and salt on medium-high speed for about 1 minute, until light and fluffy. Add the egg and flour and beat until blended. Refrigerate for about 1 hour, or until firm.

4 To make the fruit filling, in a large bowl, combine the granulated and brown sugars and the flour, salt, nutmeg, and black pepper and stir until blended. Add the peaches, blueberries, lemon zest, lemon juice, and vanilla. Toss until the fruit is evenly coated.

(RECIPE CONTINUES)

blueberry crostata

FOR THE FRUIT FILLING

¼ cup granulated sugar

¼ cup (packed) dark brown sugar

2 tablespoons all-purpose flour

Pinch of kosher salt

Pinch of freshly grated nutmeg

Pinch of coarsely ground black pepper

1¼ pounds firm-ripe fresh freestone peaches, washed and dried, pitted, and each cut into 6 wedges

½ pint fresh blueberries, washed and dried

1 tablespoon finely grated lemon zest

4½ teaspoons fresh lemon juice

½ teaspoon vanilla bean paste or pure vanilla extract

FOR THE TOPPING

1 extra-large egg

1 tablespoon milk or water

¼ cup turbinado sugar

5 Put a large piece of parchment paper (or two taped together) on a work surface. Put the dough in the center of the paper and top with a second sheet of parchment paper (or two taped together). Roll the dough into a 14-inch round about ¼ inch thick, stopping occasionally to peel away the paper, dust the dough lightly with flour, and reposition the paper so you don't get any wrinkles.

6 Scrape the chilled frangipane onto the center of the dough, and using an offset spatula, spread it in an even layer, leaving a 1½-inch border of dough.

7 Leaving any juices in the bowl, arrange the fruit in the center of the frangipane, leaving about a 2-inch border of frangipane.

8 For the topping, combine the egg and milk in a small bowl and mix with a fork until blended. Using a small pastry brush, brush the dough border with the beaten egg mixture. Fold the edges (including the part with the frangipane) over the filling, pleating the dough in evenly spaced folds as you go around and gently pressing down on the pleats to seal. The dough will not cover all the fruit filling. Brush the dough with the beaten egg mixture and sprinkle with the turbinado sugar.

9 Refrigerate the crostata for about 1 hour, until the dough is very firm, or for up to 4 hours.

10 Position a rack at the bottom of the oven, and preheat the oven to 375°F (350°F if using a convection oven). Line a large baking pan with 1-inch-high sides with parchment paper.

11 Set crostata on the baking sheet and bake for 15 minutes (12 minutes if using a convection oven), then reduce the oven temperature to 350°F (325°F if using a convection oven). Bake for 25 to 27 more minutes (24 to 26 minutes if using a convection oven), or until the crust is a deep golden brown. Transfer the baking sheet to a wire rack and let cool slightly or completely before serving.

This recipe may seem daunting, but it doesn't have to be. Everything can be made in advance and stored in the fridge. Even the unbaked finished crostata can sit in the fridge overnight.

Nectarines, apricots, blackberries, huckleberries—they are all interchangeable here. Choose the combination that you like at the height of each fruit's season.

chocolate cake with coconut, cardamom, + curry

SERVES 12 The flavors of this cake may sound a little outside the box, but at the end of the day, the cake is amazing. I wanted it to be special, with soft undertones of spices, and using Indian ones always feels exotic. The flavors intensify the longer the cake sits, so plan on making this ahead. I love serving this cake with Peanut Butter Curry Ice Cream (page 156) or with a spoonful of crème fraîche.

½ cup natural dark cocoa powder (preferably Valrhona)

¾ teaspoon ground cardamom

½ teaspoon mild curry powder

¼ teaspoon kosher salt

8 ounces bittersweet chocolate (preferably Valrhona Caraïbe 66%), chopped

½ cup (1 stick) unsalted butter, cut into 6 pieces

5 extra-large eggs, at room temperature

½ cup sugar

1 teaspoon vanilla bean paste or pure vanilla extract

½ teaspoon pure coconut extract

1 Position a rack in the middle of the oven and preheat the oven to 325°F (300°F if using a convection oven). Line the bottom of a 10-inch springform pan with parchment paper and lightly grease the sides and the paper (preferably with Pam).

2 Sift the cocoa powder, cardamom, curry powder, and salt together.

3 In a large heatproof bowl, melt the chocolate and butter over simmering water. Remove the bowl from the heat, add the cocoa mixture, and whisk until blended.

4 Using an electric mixer fitted with the whisk attachment, whip the eggs, sugar, and vanilla and coconut extracts on medium-high speed for about 4 minutes, until pale and very thick (the batter will form a ribbon when the beater is lifted). Pour into the chocolate mixture and fold until just blended. Pour the mixture into the prepared pan and spread it evenly.

5 Bake for 25 to 28 minutes (22 to 24 minutes if using a convection oven), or until the center of the cake jiggles slightly when the pan is gently shaken. Transfer the pan to a wire rack and let cool completely. Cover and refrigerate overnight or for up to 3 days.

6 Take the cake out of the fridge 1 hour before serving. Run a knife between the cake and the pan, then unclasp and remove the outer ring. Put a rack or a flat plate on top of the cake and invert the cake. Lift off the metal bottom and carefully peel away the parchment paper. Place a flat serving plate on the cake and invert one last time.

7 To serve, use a large knife dipped in hot water and wiped dry to cut the cake into slices, dipping the knife in hot water and wiping dry in between cuts.

VARIATION
Around the holidays, I like to make this cake using 1¼ teaspoons of a combination of cinnamon, nutmeg, ginger, and cloves instead of the curry and cardamom.

carrot cake cupcakes

MAKES 6 JUMBO CUPCAKES Inspired by one of my favorite cakes of all time, these are really more like small-format cakes. I don't generally love the word *cupcake,* but as these are baked individually and are definitely not muffins, *cupcake* makes sense here. Life is too short to eat bad cake, so eat the good stuff.

FOR THE FILLING

⅓ cup granulated sugar

1 tablespoon all-purpose flour

⅓ cup heavy cream

3 tablespoons unsalted butter, cut into 3 pieces

⅓ cup coarsely chopped pecans

½ teaspoon vanilla bean paste or pure vanilla extract

FOR THE CUPCAKES

1 cup all-purpose flour

1 teaspoon ground cinnamon

1 teaspoon baking powder

½ teaspoon baking soda

½ teaspoon kosher salt

⅔ cup canola or vegetable oil

1 cup granulated sugar

2 extra-large eggs, at room temperature

2 cups (lightly packed) shredded carrots

⅓ cup chopped pecans

⅓ cup dried currants

1 teaspoon vanilla bean paste or pure vanilla extract

1 To make the filling, in a small saucepan, combine the granulated sugar and flour and stir until well blended. Add the cream and butter, turn the heat on medium, and cook, stirring, until the butter is melted and the mixture is just boiling, about 5 minutes. Reduce the heat to low and simmer, whisking occasionally, for 10 minutes, or until the mixture is very thick and no longer tastes of flour. Remove the pan from the heat and let the mixture cool, stirring occasionally, until it reaches room temperature. Add the pecans and vanilla and stir until blended. Cover and refrigerate until very cold, about 2 hours.

2 To make the cupcakes, position a rack in the middle of the oven, and preheat the oven to 350°F (325°F if using a convection oven). Lightly grease (preferably with Pam) and flour a 6-cup extra-large muffin tin (each cup is 3½ × 1¾ inches).

3 Sift the flour, cinnamon, baking powder, baking soda, and salt together.

4 Using an electric mixer fitted with the paddle attachment, beat the oil and sugar on medium speed for about 30 seconds, until blended. Scrape down the sides of the bowl. Add half the flour mixture and beat on low speed until just combined. Add 1 egg and beat until blended. Add the remaining flour mixture and mix until just combined. Add the remaining egg and beat until just combined. Add the carrots, pecans, currants, and vanilla and mix until combined.

FOR THE FROSTING

4 ounces cream cheese, at room temperature

½ cup (1 stick) unsalted butter, at room temperature

2 cups confectioners' sugar

½ teaspoon vanilla bean paste or pure vanilla extract

¼ teaspoon kosher salt

¾ cup shredded coconut

5 Divide the batter evenly among the prepared muffin cups and bake for 23 to 25 minutes (15 to 17 minutes if using a convection oven), until a toothpick inserted in the center of one cupcake comes out clean. Transfer the muffin tin to a wire rack and let cool completely.

6 To make the frosting, using an electric mixer fitted with the paddle attachment, beat the cream cheese and butter on medium speed for about 2 minutes, until soft and smooth. Add the confectioners' sugar, vanilla, and salt and beat on medium-high speed for 2 minutes, until smooth, light, and fluffy.

7 Using a small sharp knife, cut a 1½-inch circle into the top of one cupcake. Cut around the circle on an angle into the cake until you reach the middle. Carefully pull out the "plug" you have just cut—it will be shaped a bit like a cone. Cut off and reserve the top of the plug and snack on the rest. Repeat with the remaining cupcakes.

8 Spoon about 1 tablespoon of the filling into the hole in each cupcake and replace the tops. Frost the cupcakes and top with the shredded coconut.

9 Serve immediately or store in an airtight container for up to 3 days.

every frozen

thing

coffee + toffee

peanut butter
curry

bacon
maple + pecan

black licorice

vanilla ice cream

MAKES ABOUT 1 QUART As a kid growing up, you were either a chocolate or a vanilla eater. Vanilla always took top billing at my house, much to the chagrin of my brother Steven. He was a chocoholic and hated vanilla. To me, nothing speaks of summer like a bowl of this ice cream and freshly picked strawberries, but it's really the perfect canvas for any ripe seasonal fruit.

My vanilla ice cream is loaded with vanilla beans. In most of my recipes, I give you the option of using vanilla bean paste or vanilla extract, but not in this recipe. Vanilla beans add so much flavor that it would be a crime not to use them. Ice creams just won't taste the same using vanilla paste or extract, which can contain artificial coloring, water, sugar, and vanillin (or should I say ethylvanillin). I really want you to experience the full, big vanilla flavor that you can only get from using the bean.

1½ cups heavy cream

1½ cups whole milk

½ teaspoon kosher salt

4 vanilla beans, split (see note, page 107)

7 extra-large egg yolks, at room temperature

¾ cup sugar

1 In a medium saucepan, combine the heavy cream, milk, and salt. Scrape all the seeds from the vanilla beans, and add them to the saucepan along with the beans. Cook over medium heat until just barely boiling, about 5 minutes. Remove the pan from the heat, cover, and set aside for at least 30 minutes. The longer the mixture steeps, the bigger the vanilla flavor.

2 In a medium bowl, whisk the egg yolks and sugar until blended.

3 Over medium heat, bring the cream mixture back to a simmer. While whisking constantly, slowly pour it into the yolk mixture until blended; then pour it all back into the saucepan. Cook over medium-low heat, stirring constantly with a heatproof spatula—making sure you get the sides and bottom of the saucepan—until the custard is thick enough to coat the spatula and to hold a line drawn through it with your finger, about 3 to 5 minutes.

(RECIPE CONTINUES)

I use a lot of vanilla beans in all my ice creams, but more so in this one. I love working with Tahitian beans. They are a bit shorter and plumper than other types of beans and are filled with lots of flavor.

I realize buying vanilla beans may be expensive, but take into account that they can be repurposed. Consider this: After you've fished them from the custard, give them a quick rinse and spread them on a baking sheet. Bake at 200°F for 1 hour, or until they are brittle. Remove from the oven and allow to cool to room temperature.

Break the beans up, put them in a spice grinder or blender, and whiz away until they become beautiful vanilla dust. Sift out any of the large pieces and regrind. Resift and discard any larger pieces. Store in an airtight container at room temperature for up to 3 weeks.

To make vanilla sugar, combine 2 cups sugar with 1 teaspoon vanilla dust. Use just as you would regular granulated sugar in recipes where you want that extra pop of vanilla flavor. I especially love vanilla sugar in cookies, ice creams, and coffee cake. Yum!

4 Pour the custard through a fine-mesh strainer into a bowl. Fish out the vanilla beans, scraping any remaining custard and seeds back into the custard, and set the beans aside (see note, left).

5 Chill the mixture in the fridge until very cold, about 1 hour, or for faster chilling, set the bowl over a larger one filled with ice and a little water. Either way, stir frequently. The chilled custard can be covered and refrigerated up to 2 days before churning.

6 To churn, pour the chilled custard into an ice cream maker and process according to the manufacturer's instructions. Serve immediately, or for a firmer ice cream, scrape into a chilled bowl, cover, and freeze until firm, or for up to 3 days.

VARIATION

Chocolate Chip Ice Cream: Melt 4 ounces bittersweet chocolate. Using a fork, drizzle the chocolate into the ice cream during the last minute or two of churning. The chocolate will harden immediately once it comes in contact with the frozen ice cream. The result is delicious shards of chocolate (not rock-hard chips) scattered throughout your ice cream that will melt in your mouth.

salted caramel

ice cream

MAKES ABOUT 1 QUART Caramel sauce and I share a love-hate relationship that has been going on for years—it is delicious to eat but can be challenging to make. My advice when making caramel is to have no distractions and a large-enough pot, because the caramel will surprise you by bubbling and splashing when you add the heavy cream and milk. But don't let that scare you off! This recipe is really easy to make.

1½ cups heavy cream

1½ cups whole milk

¾ teaspoon kosher salt

2 vanilla beans, split (see note, page 107)

¾ cup sugar

7 extra-large egg yolks, at room temperature

1 In a medium saucepan, combine the heavy cream, milk, and salt. Scrape all the seeds from the vanilla beans, and add them to the saucepan along with the beans. Cook over medium heat until just barely boiling, about 5 minutes. Remove the pan from the heat, cover, and set aside for at least 30 minutes.

2 Over medium heat, bring the cream mixture back to a simmer and keep warm.

3 In a separate large saucepan, combine the sugar and ¼ cup water, and cook over low heat, stirring occasionally, until the sugar is dissolved and the liquid is clear, about 3 minutes. Increase the heat to medium high, and cook without stirring until the sugar begins to turn golden brown on the edges, about 3 minutes. While gently swirling the pan over the heat to even out the color, cook for 4 to 6 minutes, or until the sugar turns a deep amber.

4 Slide the pan from the heat and carefully add the warm cream mixture. Please be careful, as it will steam up. Whisk until well blended and the caramel is dissolved.

(RECIPE CONTINUES)

salted caramel

5 In a medium bowl, whisk the egg yolks until blended. While whisking constantly, slowly pour the warm cream mixture into the yolk mixture until blended; then pour it all back into the saucepan. Cook over medium-low heat, stirring constantly with a heatproof spatula—making sure you get the sides and bottom of the saucepan—until the custard is thick enough to coat the spatula and to hold a line drawn through it with your finger, about 3 to 5 minutes.

6 Pour the custard through a fine-mesh strainer into a medium bowl. Fish out the vanilla beans, scraping any remaining custard and seeds back into the custard, and set the beans aside (see note, page 148). Give the custard a taste. The salt should be pronounced, so if it's not, add a few extra pinches.

7 Chill the mixture in the fridge until very cold, about 2 hours, or for faster chilling, set the bowl over a larger one filled with ice and a little water. Either way, stir frequently. The chilled custard can be covered and refrigerated up to 2 days before churning.

8 To churn, pour the chilled custard into an ice cream maker and process according to the manufacturer's instructions. Serve immediately, or for a firmer ice cream, scrape into a chilled bowl, cover, and freeze until firm, or for up to 3 days.

strawberry buttermilk ice cream

MAKES ABOUT 1 QUART We're lucky down here in South Florida, where strawberry season begins when the rest of the country is digging out from under mountains of snow. In season, I go through a ton of strawberries for my desserts. And why wouldn't I? Our berries always make great desserts because they're so flavorful. I love highlighting fresh strawberries in ice cream—and in fact, this ice cream was my mom's favorite. I always think of her when I make it.

1 pint fresh strawberries, washed, dried, hulled, and chopped

¾ cup sugar

1½ tablespoons fresh lemon juice

1 cup heavy cream

½ cup whole milk

2 tablespoons buttermilk powder (see note, facing page)

½ teaspoon kosher salt

2 vanilla beans, split (see note, page 107)

4 extra-large egg yolks

½ cup buttermilk (not low-fat)

1 In a small bowl, combine the strawberries, ¼ cup of the sugar, and the lemon juice. Refrigerate, stirring occasionally, for 1 hour, until the berry juices are released.

2 In a medium saucepan, combine the heavy cream, milk, buttermilk powder, and salt. Scrape all the seeds from the vanilla beans, and add them to the saucepan along with the beans. Cook over medium heat until just barely boiling, about 5 minutes. Remove the pan from the heat, cover, and set aside for at least 30 minutes. The longer the mixture steeps, the bigger the vanilla flavor.

3 In a medium bowl, whisk the egg yolks and the remaining ½ cup sugar until blended (the mixture will be thick).

4 Over medium heat, bring the cream mixture back to a simmer. While whisking constantly, slowly pour it into yolk mixture until blended; then pour it all back into the saucepan. Cook over medium-low heat, stirring constantly with a heatproof spatula—making sure you get the sides and bottom of the saucepan—until the custard is thick enough to coat the spatula and to hold a line drawn through it with your finger, about 3 to 5 minutes.

5 Pour the custard through a fine-mesh strainer into a bowl. Fish out the vanilla beans, scraping any remaining custard and seeds back into the custard, and set the beans aside (see note, page 148).

6 Chill the mixture in the fridge until very cold, about 2 hours, or for faster chilling, set the bowl over a larger one filled with ice and a little water. Either way, stir frequently.

7 Add the buttermilk and the strawberry mixture, and using an immersion blender, purée until smooth. If you don't have an immersion blender, whiz the strawberries in a blender or food processor before stirring them into the custard along with the buttermilk. The chilled custard can be covered and refrigerated up to 2 days before churning.

8 To churn, pour the chilled custard into an ice cream maker and process according to the manufacturer's instructions. Serve immediately, or for a firmer ice cream, scrape into a chilled bowl, cover, and freeze until firm, or for up to 3 days.

I like using berries that are somewhat past their prime. They tend to be juicier and more flavorful.

Buttermilk powder is dehydrated and concentrated buttermilk. It adds a velvety quality as well as a tangy flavor. It can be found in the supermarket next to the powdered milk.

ice cream

MAKES ABOUT 1 QUART I love all things licorice flavored, like fennel, anise, and absinthe. With a sophisticated, mysterious, and complex flavor profile, licorice is one of those things that draws a line in the sand—people either love it or hate it. That said, even licorice haters have crossed over to love this intriguing ice cream.

1⅓ cups heavy cream

1⅓ cups whole milk

½ teaspoon kosher salt

3 ounces all-natural black licorice (preferably organic), finely chopped

2 vanilla beans, split (see note, page 107)

7 extra-large egg yolks, at room temperature

½ cup sugar

1 tablespoon pastis or Pernod

1 In a medium saucepan, combine the heavy cream, milk, and salt. Add the licorice. Scrape all the seeds from the vanilla beans, and add them to the saucepan along with the beans. Cook over medium heat until just barely boiling, about 5 minutes. Remove the pan from the heat, cover, and set aside for at least 30 minutes, stirring occasionally to melt the candy. Don't worry if some little bits don't melt.

2 In a medium bowl, whisk the egg yolks and sugar until blended.

3 Over medium heat, bring the cream mixture back to a simmer. While whisking constantly, slowly pour it into the yolk mixture until blended; then pour it all back into the saucepan. Cook over medium-low heat, stirring constantly with a heatproof spatula—making sure you get the sides and bottom of the saucepan—until the custard is thick enough to coat the spatula and to hold a line drawn through it with your finger, about 3 to 5 minutes.

4 Pour the custard through a fine-mesh strainer into a bowl. Fish out the vanilla beans, scraping any remaining custard and seeds back into the custard, and set the beans aside (see note, page 148). Add the pastis.

5 Chill the mixture in the fridge until very cold, about 2 hours, or for faster chilling, set the bowl over a larger

one filled with ice and a little water. Either way, stir frequently. The chilled custard can be covered and refrigerated up to 2 days before churning.

6 To churn, pour the chilled custard into an ice cream maker and process according to the manufacturer's instructions. Serve immediately, or for a firmer ice cream, scrape into a chilled bowl, cover, and freeze until firm, or for up to 3 days.

I love eating this ice cream with Pumpkin Streusel Brioche Bread Pudding (page 118). The licorice flavor works well with any warm apple or pear dessert, as well as with fresh figs and rhubarb.

peanut butter curry ice cream

MAKES ABOUT 1 QUART I'm a risk taker when it comes to desserts. This flavor sits on the fence, with one foot in savory and one foot in sweet. It is not for the faint of heart but really is quite delicious. Blurring the lines between sweet and savory is something I like to do, and I figured if this combo of nuts, curry, and cream can work for Indian and Middle Eastern savory dishes, then why not for dessert? If after trying this ice cream, you're not convinced, then melt it down and pour it over tandoori chicken.

2 cups heavy cream

⅔ cup whole milk

2 vanilla beans, split (see note, page 107)

⅔ cup granulated sugar

½ cup creamy peanut butter (preferably organic), at room temperature

2 tablespoons (firmly packed) dark brown sugar

¾ to 1 teaspoon curry powder (see note, facing page)

½ teaspoon kosher salt

1 In a medium saucepan, combine the heavy cream and milk. Scrape all the seeds from the vanilla beans, and add them to the saucepan along with the beans. Add the granulated sugar, peanut butter, brown sugar, ¾ teaspoon curry powder, and salt. Cook, whisking constantly, over medium heat for about 4 minutes, or until mixture is smooth and almost boiling.

2 Slide the pan from the heat and give the mixture a taste. The curry flavor should be pronounced; it will mellow slightly when chilled. Go ahead and add ¼ teaspoon more if you'd like.

3 Pour the mixture into a large bowl and chill in the fridge until very cold, about 2 hours, or for faster chilling, set the bowl over a larger one filled with ice and a little water. Either way, stir frequently. The chilled custard can be covered and refrigerated up to 2 days before churning.

4 Fish out the vanilla beans, scraping any remaining custard back into the bowl, and set the beans aside (see note, page 000). To churn, pour the chilled mixture into an ice cream maker and process according to the manufacturer's instructions. Serve immediately, or for a firmer ice cream, scrape into a chilled bowl, cover, and freeze until firm, or for up to 3 days.

VARIATIONS

Peanut Butter Coconut Curry: Substitute the same amount of coconut milk for the whole milk, and add ¼ teaspoon natural coconut extract.

Ginger, Peanut Butter + Curry: Add 2 tablespoons fresh ginger juice (grate fresh ginger and squeeze out its juice) along with the curry powder.

I use a very special curry powder from southern India called *vadouvan.* It's the French version of Indian masala and is loaded with cardamom, fenugreek, fresh curry leaves, nutmeg, and cloves.

All ice creams and gelatos do not churn for the same amount of time. Those that have a higher fat content, like this one, will churn faster, so keep your eyes peeled, and stop churning as soon as the ice cream is smooth and thickened. You definitely don't want to go too far with these, as you'll end up with ice cream that looks grainy and more like overwhipped heavy cream than ice cream.

lemon ice

MAKES ABOUT 1 QUART On the summer days when my mom was working, my older brother, Steven, would take me to Max Meyers playground (my childhood favorite) in Philly. The problem was, though, that he being a teenage boy and I, well, just a little girl, he definitely wasn't interested in hanging out with me. So Steven would buy me a lemon water ice, along with a soft, mustard-topped pretzel, and then take off with his friends for hours.

Yum. I remember the tartness of the lemon ice and squeezing my cheeks and lips together before I swallowed. Oh, and those little pieces of lemon rind! I don't remember being scared of being alone, but I will never forget that flavor. It ended up that being left alone was a delicious thing.

⅔ cup sugar

1 tablespoon agave nectar

Pinch of kosher salt

1 cup fresh lemon juice

3 tablespoons finely
   grated lemon zest

1 In a medium saucepan, combine 2 cups water with the sugar, agave, and salt. Cook, stirring, over medium heat until just boiling and the sugar is dissolved, about 3 minutes. Stir in the lemon juice and zest.

2 Chill the mixture in the fridge, or for faster chilling, set the bowl over a larger one filled with ice and a little water. Either way, stir frequently. The chilled mixture can be covered and refrigerated up to 2 days before churning.

3 To churn, pour the chilled mixture into an ice cream maker and process according to the manufacturer's instructions. Serve immediately, or for a firmer ice, scrape into a chilled bowl, cover, and freeze until firm, or for up to 3 days.

ice cream

MAKES ABOUT 1 QUART I think this ice cream could qualify as breakfast. It's so salty, sweet, smoky, and nutty that you'll crave it all times of the day. It tastes great served on top of Peanut Butter Fudge Brownies (page 61).

1½ cups pure maple syrup (preferably Grade B from Vermont)

1⅓ cups whole milk

1⅓ cups heavy cream

½ teaspoon kosher salt

2 vanilla beans, split (see note, page 107)

7 extra-large egg yolks, at room temperature

1 tablespoon bourbon (preferably Maker's Mark)

3 ounces bacon (about 4 strips)

⅔ cup chopped pecans

1 In a large saucepan set over medium heat, bring the maple syrup to a boil. Reduce the heat to medium low and boil for 10 to 12 minutes, or until reduced to ¾ cup. Keep an eye on the pot, and reduce the heat if the syrup threatens to boil over.

2 Add the milk, heavy cream, and salt to the pan and whisk until blended. Scrape all the seeds from the vanilla beans, and add them to the saucepan along with the beans. Cook over medium heat until just barely boiling, about 3 minutes. Remove the pan from the heat, cover, and set aside for at least 30 minutes. The longer the mixture steeps, the bigger the vanilla flavor.

3 In a medium bowl, whisk the egg yolks until blended.

4 Over medium heat, bring the cream mixture back to a simmer. While whisking constantly, slowly pour it into the yolk mixture until blended; then pour it all back into the saucepan. Cook over medium-low heat, stirring constantly with a heatproof spatula—making sure you get the sides and bottom of the saucepan—until the custard is thick enough to coat the spatula and to hold a line drawn through it with your finger, about 3 to 5 minutes.

5 Pour the custard through a fine-mesh strainer into a bowl. Fish out the vanilla beans, scraping any remaining custard and seeds back into the custard, and set the beans aside (see note, page 148). Add the bourbon. Keep the custard at room temperature.

6 Meanwhile, in a medium skillet over medium-low heat, cook the bacon, turning to cook evenly, for about 5 minutes, or until crisp. Reserving the fat in the skillet, lift out the bacon strips and let them drain on paper towels. Let them cool and then crumble them into small pieces (think bacon bits—you'll have about ¼ cup).

7 Add the pecans to the skillet with the reserved bacon fat. Cook, stirring, over medium heat for 3 minutes, or until the nuts are toasted. Transfer the nuts to the paper towels to cool with the bacon, and spoon any remaining bacon fat into the custard.

8 To churn, pour the custard into an ice cream maker and process according to the manufacturer's instructions. Just before the ice cream is ready, add the bacon pieces and pecans and churn until blended. Serve immediately, or for a firmer ice cream, scrape into a chilled bowl, cover, and freeze until firm, or for up to 3 days.

 I like cooking with thick-sliced bacon. It yields more bacon after the fat renders, so you get more bang for your buck. You can shop online at various sites for amazing varieties. Try unique wood-smoked flavors. There is even a bacon-of-the-month club!

buttered popcorn

MAKES ABOUT 1 QUART I've given up meals for a tub of movie theater popcorn. I love the flavor so much, I had to create a gelato version. This gelato is so unique that I actually served it as a side dish for a hamburger at the Food Network South Beach Wine & Food Festival's famous Burger Bash. My popcorn ice cream sandwich was the belle of the Burger Ball. Oh, and the popcorn must be freshly made—don't even think about store-bought or the microwave variety. Sure, it might be faster, but the gelato will taste terrible!

3 cups heavy cream, plus extra if needed

1½ cups whole milk

1 cup sugar

1 teaspoon kosher salt

14 cups freshly popped popcorn (triple the recipe on page 53 and cook in 2 batches)

4 extra-large egg yolks

1 In a very large saucepan, combine the heavy cream, milk, ⅓ cup of the sugar, and the salt. Cook, whisking, over medium heat until just barely boiling and the sugar is dissolved, about 4 minutes. Add the popcorn and stir until coated. Cover and set aside until cool, about 30 minutes.

2 Strain the cream through a fine-mesh strainer into a medium saucepan, firmly pressing on the popcorn with the back of a spoon to extract every last drop of flavor and cream. You should have about 3 cups of liquid. Add more cream, if needed, to come up to this amount.

3 In an electric mixer fitted with the whisk attachment, beat the egg yolks and the remaining ⅔ cup sugar on medium-high speed for 5 minutes, or until the mixture is pale and thick and forms a ribbon when the beater is lifted.

4 Over medium heat, bring the cream mixture back to a simmer. With the mixer on medium-low speed, slowly pour the mixture into the egg yolks until blended. Pour the whole mixture back into the saucepan. Cook over

(RECIPE CONTINUES)

medium-low heat, stirring constantly with a heatproof spatula—making sure you get the sides and bottom of the saucepan—until the custard is thick enough to coat the spatula and to hold a line drawn through it with your finger, about 3 to 5 minutes.

5 Pour the custard through a fine-mesh strainer into a bowl. This custard needs to be cooled at room temperature! Because of the oil, it will harden if refrigerated, and the churned gelato won't have a smooth texture but will be more like overwhipped heavy cream and have a granular texture.

6 To churn, pour the custard into an ice cream maker and process according to the manufacturer's instructions. Serve immediately, or for a firmer gelato, scrape into a chilled bowl, cover, and freeze until firm, or for up to 3 days.

VARIATION

Caramel Corn Gelato: Drizzle ¼ cup chilled Salted Caramel Sauce (page 211) into the just-churned ice cream as you pack it into the container.

tangerine campari

MAKES ABOUT 1 QUART I find inspiration everywhere, but old-fashioned hand-crafted cocktails are often my starting point. Let me set the scene. The first time I had this cocktail, I was sitting along the water in Sorrento sipping from an old-fashioned glass filled with freshly squeezed tangerine juice, Campari, and a splash of gin. Every time I sip a tangerine Negroni, I think of the gorgeous Amalfi Coast and the way the air smells like citrus. I feel fancy and special just like the way Audrey Hepburn felt in *Breakfast at Tiffany's*. If you can't find tangerine juice, ruby red grapefruit juice or blood orange juice works as well.

⅔ cup sugar

Pinch of kosher salt

1½ tablespoons finely grated tangerine zest

2½ cups fresh tangerine juice

¼ cup Campari

1 tablespoon fresh lemon juice

1 In a medium saucepan, combine ⅓ cup water with the sugar and salt. Cook, stirring, over medium heat until just boiling and the sugar is dissolved, about 4 minutes. Stir in the tangerine zest, tangerine juice, Campari, and lemon juice.

2 Chill the mixture in the fridge until very cold, about 2 hours, or for faster chilling, set the bowl over a larger one filled with ice and a little water. Either way, stir frequently. The chilled mixture can be covered and refrigerated up to 2 days before churning.

3 To churn, pour the chilled mixture into an ice cream maker and process according to the manufacturer's instructions. Serve immediately, or for a firmer sorbet, scrape into a chilled bowl, cover, and freeze until firm, or for up to 3 days.

coffee + toffee ice cream

MAKES ABOUT 1 QUART Choosing the best ingredients matters most when the entire flavor of a dish comes from one item. Please step away from coffee beans that are dull and have no aroma! Do not attempt to make this ice cream with old, flavorless ones, because you will hate the ice cream and blame me. Use only oily, dark-roasted, aromatic espresso beans. I will sleep better at night knowing that the quart of ice cream in your freezer tastes like your morning espresso, only better.

2 cups heavy cream

1 cup whole milk

½ teaspoon kosher salt

1 vanilla bean, split (see note, page 107)

1 cup dark-roasted, aromatic espresso beans

6 extra-large egg yolks

½ cup sugar

2 tablespoons Kahlúa

1 tablespoon finely ground espresso beans

⅔ cup toffee pieces (preferably Heath bar pieces)

1 In a medium saucepan, combine the heavy cream, milk, and salt. Scrape all the seeds from the vanilla bean and add them to the saucepan along with the bean and the espresso beans. Cook over medium heat until just barely boiling, about 5 minutes. Remove the pan from the heat, cover, and set aside for at least 30 minutes. The longer the mixture steeps, the bigger the coffee flavor.

2 In a medium bowl, whisk the egg yolks and sugar until blended.

3 Over medium heat, bring the cream mixture back to a simmer. While whisking constantly, slowly pour it into the yolk mixture until blended; then pour it all back into the saucepan, scraping every last drop from the bowl. Cook over medium-low heat, stirring constantly with a heatproof spatula—making sure you get the sides and bottom of the saucepan—until the custard is thick enough to coat the spatula and to hold a line drawn through it with your finger, about 3 to 5 minutes.

4 Pour the custard through a fine-mesh strainer into a bowl. Fish out the vanilla bean, scraping any remaining custard and seeds back into the custard, and set the

vanilla bean aside (see note, page 148). Set the espresso beans aside too (see note, below).

5 Chill the mixture in the fridge until very cold, about 2 hours, or for faster chilling, set the bowl over a larger one filled with ice and a little water. Either way, stir frequently. The chilled custard can be covered and refrigerated up to 2 days before churning.

6 Stir in the Kahlúa and the ground espresso beans. To churn, pour the chilled custard into an ice cream maker and process according to the manufacturer's instructions. Just before the ice cream is ready, add the toffee pieces and churn until blended.

7 Serve immediately, or for a firmer ice cream, scrape into a chilled bowl, cover, and freeze until firm, or for up to 3 days. I serve this with a drizzle of extra coffee liqueur, but it's completely up to you.

I like making espresso bark with the espresso beans I've strained out of the custard. First, rinse and dry the beans and set aside. To make the bark, just add some beans to your favorite melted chocolate and spread on a baking pan fitted with a nonstick liner. Chill the mixture until cold and then break it into pieces.

gelato

MAKES ABOUT 1 QUART Many years ago, I had the opportunity to travel throughout Spain and taste all the best foods the country has to offer. One afternoon, I tasted the many olive oils produced in the country. It was amazing to discover the subtle nuances among them. This gelato has a pure olive oil flavor that is fruity and slightly nutty. I love serving it topped with fresh strawberries drizzled with a little balsamic vinegar, or alongside Anise Almond Biscotti (page 88) or the Peach + Blueberry Crostata (page 137).

1 cup half-and-half

1 cup whole milk

½ teaspoon kosher salt

1 vanilla bean, split (see note, page 107)

3 tablespoons finely grated lemon zest

4 extra-large egg yolks

⅔ cup sugar

¾ cup extra-virgin olive oil

1 In a medium saucepan, combine the half-and-half, milk, and salt. Scrape all the seeds from the vanilla bean, and add them to the saucepan along with the bean and the lemon zest. Cook over medium heat until just barely boiling, about 5 minutes. Remove the pan from the heat, cover, and set aside for at least 30 minutes.

2 In an electric mixer fitted with the whisk attachment, beat the egg yolks and sugar on medium-high speed for 3 to 5 minutes, or until the mixture is pale and thick and forms a ribbon when the beater is lifted.

3 With the mixer on medium speed, slowly add the olive oil, and beat until blended, about 2 minutes.

4 Over medium heat, bring the half-and-half mixture back to a simmer. With the mixer on medium-low speed, slowly pour the mixture into the yolks until blended. Pour the whole mixture back into the saucepan. Cook over medium-low heat, stirring constantly with a heat-proof spatula—making sure you get the sides and bottom of the saucepan—until the custard is thick enough to coat the spatula and to hold a line drawn through it with your finger, about 3 to 5 minutes.

5 Pour the custard through a fine-mesh strainer into a bowl. Fish out the vanilla bean, scraping any remaining custard and seeds back into the custard, and set the bean aside (see note, page 148). Let the custard cool completely at room temperature. (Because of the oil, it will harden if refrigerated, and the churned gelato won't have a smooth texture.)

6 To churn, pour the cooled custard into an ice cream maker and process according to the manufacturer's instructions. Serve immediately, or for a firmer ice cream, scrape into a chilled bowl, cover, and freeze until firm, or for up to 3 days.

ricotta gelato

MAKES ABOUT 1 QUART In every city throughout the country, you can find neighborhoods filled with hardworking Italian-American families. South Philadelphia is no exception. There, you'll find two Italian bakeries—Termini Brothers and Isgro Paticceria—that make the most amazing cannoli with a homemade ricotta filling. Those fillings are the inspiration for this gelato, whose faint hint of lemon and grappa-infused raisins make me want to sing Mario Lanza songs.

1¼ cups half-and-half

½ teaspoon kosher salt

1 vanilla bean, split (see note, page 107)

3 tablespoons finely grated lemon zest

5 extra-large egg yolks

¾ cup sugar

½ cup grappa

¾ cup dark raisins

1 cup whole-milk ricotta

½ cup heavy cream

1 In a medium saucepan, combine the half-and-half and salt. Scrape all the seeds from the vanilla bean, and add them to the saucepan along with the bean and the lemon zest. Cook over medium heat until just barely boiling, about 5 minutes. Remove the pan from the heat, cover, and set aside for at least 30 minutes.

2 In an electric mixer fitted with the whisk attachment, beat the egg yolks and sugar on medium-high speed for 5 minutes, or until the mixture is pale and thick and forms a ribbon when the beater is lifted.

3 Over medium heat, bring the half-and-half mixture back to a simmer. With the mixer on medium-low speed, slowly pour the mixture into the yolks until blended. Pour the mixture back into the saucepan. Cook over medium-low heat, stirring constantly with a heatproof spatula—making sure you get the sides and bottom of the saucepan—until the custard is thick enough to coat the spatula and to hold a line drawn through it with your finger, about 3 to 5 minutes.

4 Pour the custard through a fine-mesh strainer into a bowl. Fish out the vanilla bean, scraping any remaining custard and seeds back into the custard, and set the bean aside (see note, page 148). Discard the zest.

5 Chill the mixture in the fridge until very cold, about 2 hours, or for faster chilling, set the bowl over a larger one filled with ice and a little water. Either way, stir frequently. The chilled custard can be covered and refrigerated up to 2 days before churning.

6 Meanwhile, put the grappa and raisins in a small saucepan, and cook over medium heat for 4 minutes, or until the grappa is warm and the raisins are plump. Set aside to cool completely.

7 Add the ricotta and heavy cream to the chilled ice cream base, and using an immersion blender, purée until smooth. (If you don't have an immersion blender, whiz the ricotta and heavy cream in a blender or food processor before stirring it into the custard.)

8 Pour the chilled custard into an ice cream maker, and process according to the manufacturer's instructions.

9 Just before the gelato is ready, drain the raisins (drink the grappa or save it to drizzle over the gelato), add the raisins to the gelato, and churn until blended. Serve immediately, or for a firmer ice cream, scrape into a chilled bowl, cover, and freeze until firm, or for up to 3 days.

If you are fortunate enough to live in a city with an Italian community, you probably have a resource for freshly made ricotta cheese. It's much more flavorful than supermarket varieties, so try to find the fresh stuff if you can.

bourbon sorbet

MAKES ABOUT 1 QUART Being a bourbon drinker, I think this sorbet hits the mark on so many levels. Super-rich dark chocolate plays perfectly with oak barrel–aged bourbons. Remember to choose a bourbon that you enjoy sipping as a cocktail (especially while the sorbet is turning in the ice cream machine), because the flavor will be assertive in the sorbet.

¼ cup natural dark cocoa powder (preferably Valrhona)

¼ cup sugar

Pinch of kosher salt

2 tablespoons Lyle's Golden Syrup

6 ounces bittersweet chocolate (preferably Valrhona Caraïbe 66%), chopped

3 tablespoons bourbon (preferably Marker's Mark)

1 In a medium saucepan, whisk the cocoa powder, sugar, and salt until blended. Add about ½ cup water and whisk until smooth and thick. Add 1¾ cups water and the Lyle's syrup and whisk until blended. Cook, stirring, over medium heat until just barely boiling and the sugar is dissolved, about 5 minutes.

2 Slide the pan from the heat, add the chopped chocolate and the bourbon, and stir until the chocolate is melted and the mixture is smooth.

3 Let the custard cool at room temperature. (If you chill it in the fridge, it will be too thick, and the churned sorbet will turn grainy.)

4 To churn, pour the chilled mixture into an ice cream maker and process according to the manufacturer's instructions. Serve immediately, or for a firmer sorbet, scrape into a chilled bowl, cover, and freeze until firm, or for up to 3 days.

chocolate
bourbon
sorbet

+ chipotle ice cream

MAKES ABOUT 1 QUART I love eating chocolate-covered cherries. When I was younger, I used to bite into a dozen bonbons searching for the cherry ones, putting the half-eaten ones back in their fancy wrappers, thinking that I got away with murder. This ice cream is my tribute to those little treats. At first the flavor combo may seem a little odd, but trust me. The chipotle adds a layer of smokiness that works in perfect harmony with the uber-sweet cherries and the slight bitterness of the cocoa nibs.

1⅓ cups heavy cream

1⅓ cups whole milk

¾ teaspoon kosher salt

2 vanilla beans, split (see note, page 107)

6 extra-large egg yolks, at room temperature

5 tablespoons sugar

6 ounces bittersweet chocolate (preferably Valrhona Caraïbe 66%), chopped

¼ teaspoon ground chipotle chili pepper

⅓ cup amarena cherries, drained (reserve syrup) and coarsely chopped (see note, facing page)

3 tablespoons cocoa nibs (see note, facing page)

1 In a medium saucepan, combine the heavy cream, milk, and salt. Scrape all the seeds from the vanilla beans, and add them to the saucepan along with the beans. Cook over medium heat until just barely boiling, about 5 minutes. Remove the pan from the heat, cover, and set aside for at least 30 minutes. The longer the mixture steeps, the bigger the vanilla flavor.

2 In a medium bowl, whisk the egg yolks and sugar until blended.

3 Over medium heat, bring the cream mixture back to a simmer. While whisking constantly, slowly pour it into the yolk mixture until blended. Pour the whole mixture back into the saucepan, scraping every last drop from the bowl. Cook over medium-low heat, stirring constantly with a heatproof spatula—making sure you get the sides and bottom of the saucepan—until the custard is thick enough to coat the spatula and to hold a line drawn through it with your finger, about 3 to 5 minutes.

4 Pour the custard through a fine-mesh strainer into a bowl. Fish out the vanilla beans, scraping any remaining custard and seeds back into the custard, and set the beans aside (see note, page 148). Add the chopped

chocolate and chipotle chili powder, and stir until the chocolate is melted.

5 Chill the mixture in the fridge until very cold, about 2 hours, or for faster chilling, set the bowl over a larger one filled with ice and a little water. Either way, stir frequently. The chilled custard can be covered and refrigerated up to 2 days before churning.

6 To churn, pour the chilled custard into an ice cream maker and process according to the manu-facturer's instructions. Just before the ice cream is ready, add the cherries and cocoa nibs and churn until blended.

7 Serve immediately, or for a firmer ice cream, scrape into a chilled bowl, cover, and freeze until firm, or for up to 3 days. Serve with a drizzle of the reserved cherry syrup.

Amarena cherries—rich, luxe, and full-flavored wild Italian cherries—are small, dark, and slightly on the tart side. They are grown mostly in Bologna and Modena, Italy, and then packed in extra-wonderful sugar syrup. They're so succulent and amazing. In my opinion, nothing really can compare to their flavor and texture, especially in ice cream—so much so that I can't even offer a reasonable substitute. If you can't find these in your local specialty shop, they are worth ordering online. Please do not use the "red dye # whatever" cherries—you'll be very disappointed.

Cocoa nibs pack a powerful chocolate flavor. They are dried, roasted, and crushed cacao beans. Crunchy and tender at the same, cocoa nibs have a special flavor. Use them in ice creams, cookies, cakes, and muffins.

morn

ing
sweets

lemon ricotta pancakes

MAKES 26 (2-INCH) PANCAKES Share the lemon love with these adorable silver dollar pancakes. They are delicate and just fussy enough to be a brunch contender. Don't get me wrong, they're pretty and taste delicious, but they also remind me of a New Jersey diner cook who spent a day thinking outside of the box.

3 tablespoons sugar

1 tablespoon finely grated lemon zest

1 cup whole-milk ricotta

3 extra-large eggs, separated and at room temperature

¼ teaspoon kosher salt

½ cup all-purpose flour

Fresh fruit, for garnish

Confectioners' sugar, for garnish

Personally, I adore these cakes grilled up as silver dollars, but you can cook them up in whatever size you like—the cooking time will be just about the same. If you are feeding a crowd, go ahead and double or triple the recipe, but for the lightest, fluffiest pancakes, use the batter right away. They are also delicious with a few tablespoons of diced Candied Grapefruit Peel (page 207).

1 In a medium bowl, combine the sugar and lemon zest, and using your hands, rub them together to release the lemon oils. Add the ricotta, egg yolks, and salt, and whisk until blended. Add the flour and whisk until blended.

2 In a separate bowl, using an electric mixer fitted with the whisk attachment, beat the egg whites on medium-high speed for about 3 minutes, until they form medium-firm peaks. Scoop about one-third of the whites into the egg mixture, and using a rubber spatula, fold them in until blended. Add the remaining whites and gently fold them in until just blended. Don't stir, or the batter will deflate and leave you with flat, rubbery pancakes.

3 Lightly grease a griddle (preferably with Pam) and set it over medium heat until hot. Spoon about 2 tablespoons of batter (or, for larger cakes, up to ¼ cup) per pancake onto the griddle, about 2 inches apart. Cook for 2 to 3 minutes, or until the bottoms of the pancakes are golden or "blond" and the edges look set. Using a wide spatula, turn the pancakes and continue cooking for about 2 to 3 minutes, or until the bottoms are golden and the top springs back when lightly pressed. Repeat with the remaining batter, lightly greasing the griddle between batches.

4 Serve immediately with fresh fruit and a dusting of confectioners' sugar.

scones

MAKES 8 SCONES These scones steal the show. Period. It's funny that this simple, basic recipe has been one of the most sought-after of my career. I just smile when asked for the secret to making these just-sweet-enough scones so perfect. Don't overwork the dough, and the "secret" for light, flaky scones becomes yours. They are incredibly easy to make, even with a moment's notice.

FOR THE SCONES

1⅔ cups all-purpose flour

2 tablespoons granulated sugar

2 teaspoons baking powder

¼ teaspoon kosher salt

½ cup (1 stick) unsalted butter, cut into 8 pieces and very cold

½ cup chopped dried fruit (cherries, apricots, currants—really any dried fruit or a combination of several)

3 tablespoons half-and-half

1 extra-large egg, at room temperature

1 extra-large egg yolk

½ teaspoon vanilla bean paste or pure vanilla extract

1 Position a rack in the center of the oven, and preheat the oven to 375°F (350°F if using a convection oven). Line a baking sheet with parchment paper or a nonstick liner.

2 Using an electric mixer fitted with the paddle attachment, combine the flour, sugar, baking powder, and salt. Mix on medium-low speed for about 1 minute, or until well blended. Add the cold butter pieces and mix on medium-low speed for about 3 minutes, or until the largest pieces of butter are about pea size. Add the dried fruit and mix until combined.

3 In a small bowl, combine the half-and-half, egg, egg yolk, and vanilla, and whisk until blended.

4 With the mixer on medium-low speed, slowly add the egg mixture to the flour mixture. Mix for 1 to 2 minutes, or until just combined. The dough will be partially mixed, with a little flour remaining on the bottom of the bowl.

5 Scrape the dough and any remaining floury bits onto a work surface, and knead a few times, until it all just comes together. Do not overwork the dough, or the scones will be tough.

(RECIPE CONTINUES)

FOR THE TOPPING

1 extra-large egg beaten with 1 tablespoon milk or water

¼ cup turbinado sugar

6 Shape the dough into a 7-inch round about 1 inch thick. Using a sharp knife, cut the round into 8 wedges. Arrange the wedges about 2 inches apart on the prepared baking sheet.

7 Brush the tops of the scones with the beaten egg and milk, and sprinkle with the turbinado sugar.

8 Bake for 16 to 18 minutes (12 to 15 minutes if using a convection oven), or until the tops of the scones are deep golden brown. Transfer the baking sheet to a wire rack and let cool. Serve warm or at room temperature with Rhubarb-Blackberry Compote (page 209).

sour cream

SERVES 12 I grew up in a coffee cake–obsessed home. Is that so weird? Teething on the finest Entenmann's and Drake's, I have earned the title of "connoisseur of everything coffee cake." This is not my mom's store-bought stuff, however. It's a killer breakfast treat I know my mom would love.

FOR THE STREUSEL

¾ cup (packed) dark brown sugar

¾ cup coarsely chopped walnuts

5 ounces bittersweet chocolate (preferably Valrhona Caraïbe 66%), chopped into ½-inch pieces

4 teaspoons ground cinnamon (preferably Saigon, see note, page 69)

1 tablespoon finely ground espresso beans

FOR THE CAKE

2¼ cups all-purpose flour

1½ teaspoons baking powder

¼ teaspoon baking soda

¾ teaspoon kosher salt

½ cup (1 stick) unsalted butter, at room temperature

1 cup granulated sugar

2 extra-large eggs, at room temperature

1½ teaspoons vanilla bean paste or pure vanilla extract

1 cup sour cream, at room temperature

1 To make the streusel, combine the brown sugar, walnuts, chocolate, cinnamon, and ground espresso in a small bowl, and stir until well blended.

2 To make the cake, position an oven rack in the middle of the oven, and preheat the oven to 325°F (325°F if using a convection oven). Line the bottom and sides of a 10-cup loaf pan with foil and grease it lightly (preferably with Pam).

3 Sift the flour, baking powder, baking soda, and salt together.

4 Using an electric mixer fitted with the paddle attachment, beat the butter on medium speed for about 3 minutes, until soft and smooth. Add the granulated sugar and beat on medium-high speed for 5 minutes, until light and fluffy. Scrape down the sides of the bowl. Add the eggs, one at a time, and beat until well blended. Add the vanilla and mix until combined. Add half of the flour mixture and beat on low speed until just combined. Add the sour cream and mix until blended, about 1 minute. Add the remaining flour mixture and mix until just combined. Do not overmix.

5 Scrape half of the batter into the prepared pan and spread it evenly. Evenly distribute half of the streusel

(RECIPE CONTINUES)

mixture over the batter. Then spoon the remaining batter evenly over the streusel, and spread it evenly. Scatter the remaining streusel evenly over the top.

6 Bake for 68 to 70 minutes (50 to 60 minutes if using a convection oven), until the topping is browned and a toothpick inserted in the center of the cake comes out clean.

7 Transfer the pan to a wire rack and let cool for 20 minutes. Lift the cake and the foil liner from the pan, peel away the foil, and return the cake to the rack to cool completely. Using a serrated knife, cut the coffee cake into 1-inch-thick slices.

banana granola muffins

MAKES 8 JUMBO MUFFINS I look at these as a portable breakfast. The crunch of the granola sets them apart from traditional banana muffins. Toast them, spread them with Chocolate-Hazelnut Smear (page 216), and top them with crumbled Candied Bacon (page 188). Yeah, that's breakfast.

1⅔ cups all-purpose flour

1¼ teaspoons baking powder

½ teaspoon baking soda

¾ teaspoon kosher salt

1 cup (2 sticks) unsalted butter, at room temperature

1½ cups sugar

⅔ cup finely ground toasted hazelnuts

2 extra-large eggs, at room temperature

1½ teaspoons vanilla bean paste or pure vanilla extract

1⅓ cups granola (preferably organic)

¾ cup sour cream

⅔ cup mashed banana (from about 2 medium very ripe bananas)

1 Position a rack in the middle of the oven, and preheat the oven to 375°F (350°F if using a convection oven). Lightly grease (preferably with Pam) and flour a 6-cup extra-large muffin tin (each cup is 3½ × 1¾ inches), or line the cups with paper or foil liners.

2 Sift the flour, baking powder, baking soda, and salt together.

3 Using an electric mixer fitted with the paddle attachment, beat the butter on medium speed for about 3 minutes, until soft and smooth. Add the sugar and ground hazelnuts, and beat on medium-high speed for 5 minutes, until light and fluffy. Scrape down the sides of the bowl. Add the eggs, one at a time, and beat until well blended. Add the vanilla, and mix until combined. Add the flour mixture, and beat on low speed until just combined. Add the granola, sour cream, and banana, and using a spatula, fold until just combined.

4 Divide the batter evenly among the prepared muffin cups. Bake for 24 to 26 minutes (20 minutes if using a convection oven), until a toothpick inserted in the center of one cupcake comes out clean.

5 Transfer the muffin tin to a wire rack and serve the muffins warm or at room temperature.

candied bacon

MAKES ¼ POUND, OR 1 CUP CHOPPED BITS   Anytime I can use bacon in my pastries, I jump at the chance. This recipe is the most perfect addition to any Sunday brunch. Salty, smoky, and sweet, it beats plain ol' bacon any day. It "meats" everyone's expectations.

½ pound thick-sliced bacon

⅓ cup (packed) dark brown sugar

¼ cup pure maple syrup (preferably organic)

2 tablespoons molasses

¼ teaspoon freshly ground black pepper

The chopped candied bacon is used in the Bacon Praline (page 212) and can be used in the Cinni Mini Bun Bites (facing page) or stirred into ice cream. You can also dice up the bacon strips and use as a garnish or topping for the Peanut Butter Curry Ice Cream (page 156).

1 In a medium bowl, combine the bacon, brown sugar, maple syrup, molasses, and pepper, and stir until the bacon is coated. Cover and refrigerate for at least 30 minutes, or for up to 24 hours.

2 Position a rack in the center of the oven, and preheat the oven to 375°F (350°F if using a convection oven). Line a large sheet pan with 1-inch-high sides with foil, and position a wire rack inside the pan.

3 Arrange the bacon strips on the rack. Bake for 28 to 30 to minutes (20 to 25 minutes if using a convection oven), or until the bacon is dark brown.

4 Transfer the pan to a wire rack, and let cool for about 10 minutes. Pry the bacon off the wire rack (yep, it will be sticky), and serve immediately, or cool completely and whiz in the food processor until it is finely chopped. Store in an airtight container in the refrigerator for up to 5 days.

MAKES 36 BITES Eating sweets at breakfast is one of the greatest guilty pleasures of all time. Cinnamon buns may just be the quintessential brunch sweet. These mini bites, which are too cute for words, are awesome just the way they are, but please try them with Bacon Praline (page 212) folded into the filling. It's pretty amazing. Also, be sure to try them in the Cinni Mini Bun Pudding recipe (page 111). This favorite sweet is not just for breakfast anymore.

FOR THE DOUGH

1 cup whole milk

2¼ teaspoons (1 packet) instant yeast

¾ cup (1½ sticks) unsalted butter, cut into 9 pieces and at room temperature

2 extra-large eggs, at room temperature

½ cup granulated sugar

1 teaspoon kosher salt

4 cups all-purpose flour

FOR THE FILLING

1 cup (packed) dark brown sugar

1 tablespoon ground cinnamon (preferably Saigon, see note, page 69)

6 tablespoons (¾ stick) unsalted butter, very soft but not melted

1 To make the dough, in a small saucepan, heat the milk over medium heat until it registers about 125°F on an instant-read thermometer. Pour it into the bowl of a stand mixer, sprinkle the yeast over the top, and mix until blended. Add the butter, eggs, granulated sugar, and salt. Using the dough hook attachment, mix on medium speed for 1 minute, or until blended. Add the flour and mix on medium-low speed for 1 to 2 minutes, or until the flour is completely incorporated. Increase the speed to medium high, and knead until the dough is very smooth and elastic and pulls away from the bottom of the bowl (a little will stick to the sides), about 5 minutes. Scrape the sides of the bowl, scoop up the dough, and shape it into a ball.

2 Lightly grease (preferably with Pam) the sides of the same bowl, and put the dough back in. Cover the top with plastic wrap and let the dough rise in a warm spot for about 1 hour, or until doubled in size.

3 Lightly grease (preferably with Pam) a 9 × 13-inch baking pan.

4 In a small bowl, combine the brown sugar and cinnamon for the filling, and stir until well blended.

(RECIPE CONTINUES)

½ cup (1 stick) unsalted
    butter, at room
    temperature

2 ounces cream cheese,
    at room temperature

½ teaspoon vanilla bean
    paste or pure vanilla
    extract

Pinch of kosher salt

1½ cups confectioners'
    sugar

5 Scrape the dough onto a work surface, divide it into two equal pieces, and wrap one piece in plastic wrap so it doesn't dry out. Roll the dough into an 18 × 7-inch rectangle. Spread half of the butter for the filling evenly over the dough and sprinkle with half of the brown sugar mixture, and using your fingers, press it lightly into the butter.

6 Beginning on one long side, roll up the dough, jelly roll–style, pinching to seal. Position the roll, seam side down, on the work surface and cut it into 1-inch-wide pieces. Arrange the pieces, cut side up, in the prepared pan in even rows, leaving room for the other half of the dough, and cover the pan with plastic wrap. Repeat with the remaining dough and filling. Let the rolls rise in a warm spot for about 1 hour, or until doubled in size.

7 While the bites are rising, make the icing. Combine the butter, cream cheese, vanilla, and salt in a medium bowl. Using an electric mixer fitted with the paddle attachment, beat the mixture on medium speed for about 1 minute, or until smooth. Add the confectioners' sugar and beat on low speed until blended, about 1 minute. Increase the speed to medium, and beat until smooth and fluffy, about 2 minutes. Cover and set the icing aside at room temperature until ready to serve.

8 Position a rack in the center of the oven, and preheat the oven to 350°F (325°F if using a convection oven).

9 Remove the plastic from the baking pan and bake the bites for 38 to 40 minutes (25 to 30 minutes if using a convection oven), or until they are puffed and browned. Transfer the baking dish to a wire rack and cool slightly. Serve warm with a smear of the icing on each bite.

meyer lemon tea bread

SERVES 8 TO 10 Lemon desserts always take a backseat on the brunch menu to rich chocolate and gooey caramel ones, but I will go out on a limb and let everyone know I prefer this cake to just about anything I bake. Tart and sour components weave their way through my brunch repertoire. I secretly eat Sour Patch Kids and hide them in the glove compartment of my car.

FOR THE SYRUP

¾ cup sugar

½ cup fresh Meyer lemon juice

2 tablespoons finely grated Meyer lemon zest

FOR THE CAKE

1¾ cups all-purpose flour

1¼ teaspoons baking powder

¾ teaspoon kosher salt

2 extra-large eggs, at room temperature

1¼ cups sugar

3 tablespoons finely grated Meyer lemon zest

1 teaspoon vanilla bean paste or pure vanilla extract

¾ cup whole milk, at room temperature

½ cup (1 stick) unsalted butter, melted and cooled

3 tablespoons fresh Meyer lemon juice

1 To make the syrup, in a small pan, combine the sugar, juice, and zest. Cook, stirring occasionally, over medium heat until the sugar is dissolved, about 5 minutes.

2 To make the cake, position a rack in the middle of the oven and preheat the oven to 350°F (325°F if using a convection oven).

3 Lightly grease (preferably with Pam) and flour the bottom and sides of an 8½ × 4½-inch loaf pan.

4 Sift together the flour, baking powder and salt.

5 Using an electric mixer fitted with the paddle attachment, beat the eggs, sugar, zest, and vanilla on medium speed for about 1 minute, until blended. Add a third of the flour mixture and beat on low speed until just combined. Add the milk and mix until blended. Add another third of the flour mixture and mix until blended. Repeat with the butter and remaining flour. Add the lemon juice and mix until blended. Increase the speed to medium high and beat for 2½ minutes.

6 Scrape the batter into the prepared pan and spread it evenly. Bake for 64 to 66 minutes (50 minutes if using a convection oven), until the top is browned and a toothpick inserted in the center of the cake comes out clean.

7 Transfer the pan to a wire rack. Using a long, thin wooden skewer, poke the top of the cake through to the bottom in about 25 places. Brush or spoon the syrup over the top of the bread and then let it cool completely.

8 Slide a thin knife around the edges of the pan, invert the cake, lift the pan off, and turn the bread top side up.

Meyer lemons are a cross between a lemon and a mandarin orange, somewhat sweeter than a lemon. They're less tart and a bit floral, which makes them perfect for desserts. I love using them in cakes, cookies, jams, and ice creams. If you can't find Meyers for the syrup, use regular lemons, replacing 3 tablespoons of the juice with orange or blood orange juice; for the bread, use 2 tablespoons lemon juice combined with 1 tablespoon orange or blood orange juice.

panini

SERVES 6 My friend Betty invited me to a dinner party that had been planned by children staying at her home. The kids think I'm kind of a rock star because I create such yummy sweet treats, and they asked me to create a dessert that was delicious and fun for them to make. Bananas, toffee, chocolate, and caramel seemed like just the thing for them, and a panini grill not only is easy for kids to use but makes a great crunchy sandwich. It's even more fun if you let the kids drizzle these panini with Best-Ever Chocolate Sauce (page 214) or Salted Caramel Sauce (page 211).

¼ cup granulated sugar

1½ teaspoons ground cinnamon (preferably Saigon, see note, page 69)

9 large ripe bananas (not too ripe)

12 ¾-inch-thick slices brioche or challah (day-old bread works best)

6 tablespoons (¾ stick) unsalted butter, soft but not melted

¼ cup dulce de leche

3 tablespoons sweetened condensed milk

1 teaspoon fleur de sel

1 cup crushed chocolate-covered toffee pieces (preferably Heath bar)

Confectioners' sugar, for garnish

1 Position a rack in the center of the oven, and preheat the oven to 300°F (275°F if using a convection oven). Preheat a panini or sandwich press according to the manufacturer's instructions. (If you don't have a press, heat a griddle pan over medium heat until hot.) Line a large baking sheet with foil.

2 In a small bowl, combine the sugar and cinnamon, and stir until well blended. Peel the bananas, and cut each one lengthwise, then again crosswise. You'll have a total of 36 pieces.

3 Arrange the bread slices on a work surface. Spread them evenly with the butter, sprinkle with the cinnamon sugar, and then flip the slices over. Divide the dulce de leche among the slices and spread it evenly.

4 Using the tines of a fork, drizzle the sweetened condensed milk over 6 of the slices and sprinkle with the fleur de sel. Arrange 6 banana pieces on each of the 6 slices, overlapping and stacking as needed to make the bananas lie as flat and as evenly as possible. The second layer of bananas works best when arranged on a 90-degree angle in relation to the first.

(RECIPE CONTINUES)

that rock
world

+ basil compote

peach, blueberry

MAKES 3½ CUPS I love how this bright, simple compote—my favorite—makes everything taste great, gathering the best that summer has to offer. Serve it with the Lemon Meringue Tart (page 131), Lemon Ricotta Pancakes (page 179), yogurt and granola, or ice cream.

1 tablespoon finely grated orange zest

½ cup fresh orange juice

1 tablespoon finely grated lemon zest

¼ cup fresh lemon juice

3 tablespoons sugar

½ vanilla bean (see note, page 107)

½ large bunch fresh basil, washed and dried

Pinch of kosher salt

1 pound firm-ripe fresh freestone peaches, peeled, pitted, and each cut into 6 or 8 wedges

1 cup fresh blueberries, washed and dried

You can vary the fruits in this compote, but just make sure they are really ripe. Try using apricots or nectarines instead of the peaches, and raspberries or huckleberries instead of the blueberries.

1 In a medium saucepan, combine the orange zest, orange juice, lemon zest, lemon juice, and sugar. Scrape all the seeds from the vanilla bean, and add them to the saucepan along with the bean. Set aside a few nice leaves of basil, and put the remaining leaves and stems in the saucepan. Cook, stirring occasionally, over medium-high heat until boiling, about 4 minutes. Boil for 2 minutes, until the syrup is slightly thickened (you'll have about ½ cup). Remove the pan from the heat and stir in the salt.

2 In a large heatproof bowl, combine the peaches and blueberries. Pour the hot syrup over the fruit and gently toss until evenly coated. Set aside to cool completely.

3 Fish out the basil leaves and stems and vanilla bean, scraping any remaining syrup and seeds back into the compote. Set the bean aside (see note, page 148) and discard the basil. Refrigerate until cold, or for up to 1 day.

4 To serve, stack the reserved basil leaves on a cutting board, and using a chef's knife, cut into thin strips. Before serving, sprinkle the basil over the compote.

strawberry consomme

MAKES 1½ CUPS This method for extracting the full flavor of the strawberry rocks! I love this with Basil Panna Cotta (page 120) or mixed with club soda, champagne, or vodka.

4 pints fresh strawberries, washed, dried, hulled, and cut in half

¾ cup sugar

1 In a medium heatproof bowl, combine the strawberries with the sugar and ¼ cup water Stir until well blended. Cover the bowl with two or three layers of plastic wrap and one final layer of foil.

2 Set the bowl over a large pot of simmering water (the bowl should fit comfortably on top of the pan and the water should be just under the bowl but not touching), and cook for about 1 to 1½ hours, until the berries have lost their color and the syrup is ruby red. Make sure to check the water level in the pot a few times during the cooking and add more water if needed.

3 Slide the pan from the heat and carefully peel away the foil and plastic. Careful of the steam! Pour the fruit and syrup through a fine-mesh strainer into a clean bowl. Don't press on the strawberries—it will make the consommé cloudy.

4 Let the consommé cool completely. Then cover and refrigerate until chilled, or for up to 3 days.

blackberry-tarragon jam

MAKES 1 CUP This jam has a very special place in my heart. I love licorice, and tarragon has a sweet licorice and very subtle black pepper flavor that matches well with sweet-tart blackberries. I serve this jam along with Tangerine Creamsicle Pots de Crème (page 104) or Lemon Ricotta Pancakes (page 179). They were made for each other.

1 pint ripe blackberries, washed and dried

⅓ cup plus 4½ teaspoons sugar

1 large sprig fresh tarragon, washed and dried

¾ teaspoon fresh lemon juice

½ teaspoon finely grated lemon zest

2 tablespoons powdered fruit pectin

I love that the tarragon imparts a peppery flavor to the jam, but not everyone is crazy about it. Experiment with other fresh herbs: cilantro, thyme, lemongrass, and fresh ginger are also great jam mates.

1 In a medium nonreactive saucepan, combine 1 table-spoon water with the blackberries, ⅓ cup of the sugar, the tarragon, lemon juice, and lemon zest. Cook, stirring frequently, over medium-high heat until the mixture is boiling, about 3 to 5 minutes. Reduce the heat to low and simmer, stirring occasionally and pressing on the berries, for 20 minutes, or until the mixture is reduced and thickened (you'll have about 1¼ cups).

2 In a small bowl, combine the remaining 4½ teaspoons sugar and the pectin, and whisk until blended. Add to the berry mixture, and stir for 1 minute, until the sugar is dissolved.

3 Strain the mixture through a fine-mesh strainer set over a medium bowl, firmly pressing on the berries with the back of a spoon to extract every last bit of flavor and juice. Discard the seeds and tarragon.

4 Cover the surface directly with plastic wrap (this prevents a skin from forming), and set aside to cool completely. Spoon into a jar, cover, and refrigerate for up to 2 weeks.

MAKES 1½ CUPS This jam is Pop T's BFF. It's flavor-forward and can withstand the heat of an oven with excellent results. You can use all types of fruit purées: mango, black mission fig, raspberry, tangerine, and strawberry are some of my favorites.

1¼ cups sugar

½ cup unsweetened fruit purée

1 pouch (3 ounces) liquid fruit pectin

1 In a medium saucepan, combine the sugar and the fruit purée. Cook, stirring frequently, over medium heat until the sugar is dissolved, about 2 minutes. Increase the heat to high, and bring to a boil, about 4 minutes. Slide the pan from the heat and add the pectin. Stir until well blended.

2 Pour into a medium bowl, and set the bowl over a large bowl filled with ice and a little water. Stir frequently (this keeps a skin from forming, and the jam will stay smooth), until the mixture is cold and has thickened.

3 Pour into a container, cover, and refrigerate for up to 2 weeks.

I like my fruit jams with seeds, but if you'd prefer seedless, no problem. Strain the purée before measuring out ½ cup and proceed as directed.

grapefruit marmalade

MAKES 1½ CUPS Eating grapefruit marmalade on a scone with a side of clotted cream and lemon curd has to be one of my favorite food memories. The Hotel del Coronado in San Diego served the grandest "high tea," elegant and sophisticated and absolutely delicious. I felt regal sipping Earl Grey tea and eating those amazing scones topped with tart marmalade.

Classic marmalade takes hours to make; my recipe is a wonderful shortcut version. The flavor magic is in the zest. I keep a jar in my fridge at all times to spread on Scones (page 180) and crumble goat cheese on top. This makes an awesome filling for Pop T's (page 12) and also tastes great with Meyer Lemon Tea Bread (page 192).

1¼ cups sugar

2 tablespoons finely grated grapefruit zest

½ cup grapefruit juice

1 pouch (3 ounces) liquid fruit pectin

¼ cup chopped Candied Grapefruit Peel (see facing page), prepared through step 4

1 In a medium saucepan, combine the sugar, grapefruit zest, and grapefruit juice. Cook over medium heat, stirring frequently, until the sugar is dissolved, about 2 minutes. Increase the heat to high, and bring to a boil, about 3 minutes. Slide the pan from the heat and add the pectin. Stir until well blended.

2 Pour into a medium bowl set over a large bowl filled with ice and a little water. Stir frequently (this keeps a skin from forming and the jam will stay smooth) until the mixture is cold and has thickened. Stir in the candied zest.

3 Pour into a container, cover, and refrigerate for up to 2 weeks.

MAKES ½ CUP You have options when you make this recipe. You can drain the peel and toss it in sugar as directed, or keep the peel in its sugar syrup, where it will last in the fridge for a few weeks. Dice up the peel and add it to Lemon Ricotta Pancakes (page 179), fold it into cream cheese frosting for Carrot Cake Cupcakes (page 142), and, of course, use it in Grapefruit Marmalade (facing page). Its understated elegance gives these recipes a great pop of flavor.

1 large grapefruit
1½ cups sugar

1 Using a sharp knife, cut off the top and bottom of the grapefruit, deep enough to expose the fruit. Cut the rind and the pith of the fruit top to bottom into 8 sections. Using your thumb, separate each strip of rind from the fruit. Using a small knife, cut off a thin layer of the white pith, leaving a bit remaining on the rind. Slice the peels into ¼-inch-wide strips. Reserve the grapefruit slices for another use.

2 In a medium saucepan, combine the peels with 2 cups of cold water (add more water if the peels aren't covered). Bring to a boil over high heat. Strain the peels, discarding the water, and return them to the saucepan. Cover again with 2 cups of fresh cold water, bring to a boil, and strain again. Repeat once more, for a total of three boils.

3 In the same saucepan, combine the peels, 1 cup of the sugar, and 1½ cups cold water, and bring to a boil over high heat. Reduce the heat to low and simmer gently, stirring occasionally, for

(RECIPE CONTINUES)

16 minutes, until the peels are translucent. Slide the pan from the heat and let cool completely.

4 Strain the peels (you should keep the sugar syrup to use in drinks like lemonade). If adding to Grapefruit Marmalade (page 206), use now, before drying and tossing with sugar.

5 To dry the peels, arrange a wire rack over a rimmed baking sheet, spread the peels out in an even layer on the rack, and let dry for 4 to 6 hours, or until slightly tacky.

6 Put the remaining ½ cup sugar in a small bowl, add the peels, and toss with the sugar to coat completely.

7 Store the candied peels in an airtight container in a cool, dry place for up to 1 month.

rhubarb-blackberry compote

MAKES ABOUT 3 CUPS I look forward to rhubarb season all year long! This compote is a wonderful way to showcase rhubarb's tart, summery flavor, and I think it pairs really well with blackberries. Serve this with Ricotta Gelato (page 170), Lemon Ricotta Pancakes (page 179), Scones (page 180), or Meyer Lemon Tea Bread (page 192).

¾ cup sugar

1 teaspoon finely grated lemon zest

1 pound rhubarb, washed, dried, trimmed, and cut into ¾-inch pieces

1 vanilla bean, split (see note, page 107)

2 pints fresh blackberries, washed, dried, and cut in half if very large

1 In a large saucepan, combine the sugar and lemon zest. Using your fingers, rub the zest with the sugar to release the lemon oils. Add the rhubarb and set aside, stirring occasionally, for 15 minutes, or until the mixture is juicy.

2 Scrape all the seeds from the vanilla bean and add them to the saucepan along with the bean. Cook, stirring frequently, over medium-high heat until the mixture is boiling, about 3 minutes. Reduce the heat to low, and simmer for about 5 minutes, until the rhubarb begins to break down (you want the rhubarb to still be a bit chunky).

3 Slide the pan from the heat and set aside to cool completely. Cover and refrigerate until well chilled, or for up to 1 day.

4 Fish out the vanilla bean, scraping any remaining syrup and seeds back into the compote, and set the bean aside (see note, page 148). Add the blackberries, and stir gently until coated.

5 Serve immediately, or store in the refrigerator for 2 to 3 days.

hazelnut praline

MAKES 1⅔ CUPS Though a simple recipe, hazelnut praline packs in a bunch of flavor and texture. It's basically hazelnuts and sugar cooked to a crisp caramel, then ground to a powder. Fold this into the buttercream filling for Red Velvet Twinks (page 19) and Overstuffed O's (page 47).

½ cup sugar

1 cup blanched hazelnuts, toasted

¼ teaspoon kosher salt

1 tablespoon unsalted butter, at room temperature

1 Line a baking sheet with a nonstick liner (parchment paper won't work for this). Grease the bottom of a metal spatula (preferably with Pam).

2 In a medium saucepan, combine the sugar with 1 tablespoon water, and cook over medium heat, stirring occasionally, until the sugar is dissolved and the liquid is clear, about 2 minutes. Increase the heat to medium high and bring to a boil, about 3 minutes.

3 Add the hazelnuts and salt, and cook, stirring constantly, until the sugar begins to turn brown on the edges, about 3 minutes. The sugar will look dry and granular but will melt into a caramel that coats the nuts. Continue cooking and stirring (to even out the color) for another 4 to 6 minutes, until the nuts are coated with a deep amber caramel.

4 Slide the pan from the heat and add the butter. Stir until the butter is blended.

5 Carefully and quickly pour the mixture onto the prepared baking sheet, and using the greased spatula, spread it into a thin layer.

6 Set aside at room temperature for about 1 to 2 hours, or until completely cool and hard. Break apart and process in a food processor until finally ground. Store in an airtight container for up to 2 weeks.

salted caramel

MAKES 1⅓ CUPS Caramel sauce is a staple in my pastry kitchen. I add salt to balance out the sweet caramel and to engage more areas of the taste buds. Good salt makes food taste better; great salt makes desserts extraordinary. Serve this with Coconut Custard Pie (page 126), Chocolate Bourbon Fudge Tart (page 134), Granny Smith Apple Streusel Pie (page 124), Buttered Popcorn Gelato (page 163), or Banana Toffee Panini (page 194). Actually, almost every recipe in this book would benefit from being paired with this sauce. It puts desserts in a happy place!

¾ cup heavy cream

1 to 1½ teaspoons kosher salt

1 cup sugar

1 tablespoon Lyle's Golden Syrup

¼ cup crème fraîche

4 tablespoons (½ stick) unsalted butter, cut into 4 pieces and at room temperature

1 teaspoon vanilla bean paste or pure vanilla extract

1 In a small saucepan, combine the heavy cream and 1 teaspoon of the salt. Heat over medium heat until very hot, about 3 minutes. Reduce the heat to low and keep the cream warm.

2 In a large saucepan, combine the sugar, Lyle's syrup, and ¼ cup of water, and cook over low heat, stirring occasionally, until the sugar is dissolved and the liquid is clear, about 2 minutes.

3 Increase the heat to medium high, and boil, without stirring, for 3 to 5 minutes, or until the sugar begins to turn golden brown on the edges. Gently swirl the pan over the heat to even out the color, and cook for another 2 to 3 minutes, or until the sugar turns deep amber.

4 Slide the pan from the heat, and slowly add the cream. Careful! It will splatter. Add the crème fraîche, butter, and vanilla, and whisk until well blended. Give the caramel a taste (careful, it's HOT!), and add a pinch or two more of salt, if desired.

5 Use immediately, or set aside to cool completely, cover, and refrigerate for up to 2 weeks.

6 To serve, reheat gently over simmering water, but don't let it get too hot, or it will separate.

bacon praline

MAKES ABOUT ¾ POUND Mixing salty and sweet items together is not a new concept—think Snickers candy bars, peanut butter, and even pineapple-and-ham pizza. I will admit that adding salty bacon to desserts is new for some folks, but I think this combo is brilliant. Bacon praline is one of my favorite ways to play with salty and sweet. Eat it as is. Chop it up and fold into cookie fillings like Mochaccino Whoopie Pies (page 26), Overstuffed Nutters (page 43), and especially Junk in Da Trunk (page 82). Or grind it up and add it to the Cinni Mini Bun Bites (page 189).

¾ cup sugar

½ cup coarsely chopped pecans

½ teaspoon kosher salt

1 cup chopped Candied Bacon (page 188)

2 tablespoons chilled bacon fat (or unsalted butter, at room temperature)

¼ teaspoon fleur de sel or coarse sea salt

1 Line a baking sheet with a nonstick liner (parchment paper won't work for brittle). Grease the bottom of a metal spatula (preferably with Pam).

2 In a medium saucepan, combine the sugar and 2 table-spoons water, and cook over medium heat, stirring occasionally, until the sugar is dissolved and the liquid is clear, about 2 minutes. Increase the heat to medium high and bring the mixture to a boil.

3 Add the pecans and salt, and cook, stirring constantly, until the sugar begins to turn brown on the edges. The sugar will look dry and granular but will melt into a lovely caramel. Continue cooking and stirring for another 4 to 6 minutes, until the caramel is liquid and deep amber.

4 Slide the pan from the heat, and add the bacon and bacon fat. Stir until the bacon fat is blended in and the bacon is evenly coated with the caramel.

5 Carefully and quickly pour the mixture onto the prepared baking sheet, and using the greased spatula, spread it into a thin layer. Sprinkle with the fleur de sel. Set aside at room temperature for 1 to 2 hours, or until completely cool and hard. Break into small clusters, and store in an airtight container for up to 5 days.

sauce

MAKES 1¼ CUPS Every great ice cream deserves a great chocolate sauce. Adding malted milk powder is what takes this sauce to another level. This sauce is fantastic with Banana Toffee Panini (page 194), Chocolate Cake with Coconut, Cardamom, + Curry (page 140) and the Chocolate Bourbon Fudge Tart (page 134).

1 cup heavy cream

2 tablespoons malted milk powder

½ teaspoon vanilla bean paste or pure vanilla extract

Pinch of kosher salt

6 ounces bittersweet chocolate (preferably Valrhona Caraïbe 66%), finely chopped

2 tablespoons bourbon (preferably Maker's Mark) or rum (optional)

1 In a medium saucepan, combine the heavy cream, malted milk powder, vanilla, and salt. Heat over medium heat until just boiling, about 2 minutes.

2 Slide the pan from the heat, add the chocolate and bourbon (if using), and whisk until smooth.

3 Use immediately, or set aside to cool completely, cover, and refrigerate for up to 2 weeks.

4 To serve, reheat gently over simmering water.

rum toffee sauce

MAKES 1 CUP This is the baby brother to my Salted Caramel Sauce (page 211) because it's not as thick, but it's packed with a rum kick! Serve this sauce over warm bread pudding, French toast, ice cream, or grilled pineapples. I also love adding toasted macadamia nuts and serving it with sautéed bananas over pancakes or waffles. Plus it's perfect with Coconut Custard Pie (page 126) or Sour Cream Coffee Cake (page 183).

¾ cup (packed) dark brown sugar

5 tablespoons unsalted butter, cut into 4 pieces

⅓ cup heavy cream

2 tablespoons dark rum

½ teaspoon vanilla bean paste or pure vanilla extract

¼ teaspoon kosher salt

1 In a medium saucepan, combine the brown sugar and butter. Cook over low heat, stirring occasionally, until the butter is melted and the sugar is dissolved, about 2 minutes. Increase the heat to medium high and bring to a full boil, about 3 minutes.

2 Slide the pan from the heat. Add the cream, rum, vanilla, and salt, and whisk until well blended. Give the sauce a taste (careful, it's hot!), and add a pinch or two more of salt, if desired.

3 Use immediately, or set aside to cool completely, cover, and refrigerate for up to 2 weeks.

4 To serve, reheat gently over simmering water, but don't let it get too hot, or it will separate.

chocolate-hazelnut smear

MAKES 1¼ CUPS I wish I had a dollar for every jar of Nutella I've purchased in the last ten years. This recipe comes very close to the original, and it has all-natural ingredients, too. Serve it with Banana Granola Muffins (page 186), or spread it on Junk in Da Trunk cookies (page 82) and use them to sandwich a scoop of Really Great Vanilla Ice Cream (page 146) for a high-end ice cream sandwich.

8 ounces milk chocolate (preferably Valrhona)

¾ cup skinless hazelnuts, toasted

2 tablespoons confectioners' sugar

2 tablespoons natural dark cocoa powder (preferably Valrhona)

½ teaspoon vanilla bean paste or pure vanilla extract

Pinch of kosher salt

3 tablespoons hazelnut oil

1 Melt the milk chocolate in a small heatproof bowl set over simmering water, stirring until the chocolate is melted and smooth. Remove the bowl from the heat and set aside. Combine the hazelnuts, sugar, cocoa powder, vanilla, and salt in a food processor. Process for 1 minute, or until the mixture forms a paste. Add the oil and process until blended.

2 Scrape the nut mixture into a small bowl, and add the melted chocolate. Stir until well blended. If you prefer a smooth spread, pour the warm mixture into a strainer set over a bowl, pressing on the nuts to get all of their flavor.

3 Use the spread immediately (it will be soft), or set aside to cool completely, cover, and keep at room temperature for up to 2 weeks.

If you make a smooth version of this recipe, save the chocolate-covered ground nuts, spread them on a sheet pan, and chill to make a delicious hazelnut-chocolate bark. Chop it up and put it in ice creams.